Ireland's Credit Crunch

Front cover: Famine sculpture on the banks of the Liffey. In the background towers the International Financial Services Centre.

Ireland's Credit Crunch
The costs and the alternative

Kevin Keating
Jonathan Morrison
Joe Corrigan

Resistance Press, London

Published by

Resistance Press
PO Box 62732
London
SW2 9GQ.

© 2010 Keating, Morrison, Corrigan

ISBN 978-0-902869-76-9

Kevin Keating is a trade union activist, a long -standing opponent of social partnership in the Irish Trade Union movement and advocate of rank and file organization.

Jonathan Morrison is a researcher with a wide knowledge of the political development of emerging economies.

Joe Corrigan is an accountant with a background in economics and author of "Prisoners of Social Partnership," an analysis of the corrosive effects of collaboration between the Irish government and Trade Union leadership.

Further work by all three authors and further analysis of the Irish economy can be found at:
www.socialistdemocracy.org

Contents

Introduction

We are living through surreal times, in which the Minister of Finance can claim to have launched "the cheapest bailout in the world so far" which then threatens to bankrupt the whole State. In which hundreds of thousands take pay cuts to bail out the banks while the best paid in the worst bank, Anglo–Irish, get pay increases. In which the Finance Minister one year says the banks will advise the Irish people on how to manage their finances and a year later calls for courses for bankers on how to lend to people who aren't property speculators. Taxes are increased for workers while Bertie Ahern is given tax breaks meant for artists because he (?) writes his autobiography. You couldn't make it up. You might cry if you didn't laugh. One thing you will definitely be is "mad as hell."[1]

This short book is about the economic catastrophe which has engulfed the Irish people since 2008 and what should be done about it. It is not written to make readers angry at this situation. If you are not already furious at the assault on your lives and the gross unfairness of what is happening then nothing that the authors of this book write would make a difference.

Nor is the book about whether the economic policies of the Government will work, although we do make judgements on this. By 'work' it is usually meant whether the economy will return to growth or

---

1 Mary McAleese, President of Ireland, Irish Independent, 22/05/10.

the debt burden be repaid without default or the banks returned to profitability. That this might mean growth in GDP caused by increased multinational profits but with not one additional job created (because low corporate taxation makes reporting profits in Ireland more convenient); or that it might mean stabilisation of the debt because our children do not receive a proper education, or that people die on health service waiting lists or that the elderly live and die lonely and abandoned lives with no social support; or that some banks are saved by ripping off the population through higher interest rates or by our tax and pension money. Well what sort of 'working' is this?

At the end of the day the fact that the current economic system might right itself because enough pain is inflicted on workers, the elderly, young people and the poor is reason enough to seek an alternative. When we realise that this may be our future for an indefinite period there is every reason to seek an alternative. When it is further realised that such crises are an inevitable part of the current system even the very reluctant may be compelled to agree that some radical changes may be needed.

The purpose of this book is to explain why such conclusions are warranted and what the alternative might consist of. It is not a book of euphemisms. It is not one of reserved judgement. It is a book that is confident that the socialist analysis of the current crisis is both correct and confirmed. It is also confident that what it has to say will become more and more relevant and that any weaknesses and mistakes will not be those that render it redundant but make its central argument stronger.

Chapter 1

The Crisis: You couldn't make it up

"It is possible that places like Zimbabwe have bigger contractions, but you know when you're in trouble when you're saying at least we're not Zimbabwe. You're talking about the biggest contraction in an industrialised country since the Great Depression."[2]

This is according to Alan Barrett of the Economic and Social Research Institute (ESRI). While a comparison between the economies of Zimbabwe and Ireland is clearly an exaggeration, the fact that it can be made at all gives some indication of the depth of our economic crisis. The Irish economy has suffered a contraction over a two–year period that fits the technical criteria for a depression never mind a recession and the decline is all the more devastating given that it follows a prolonged period in which the economy had recorded some of the highest growth rates anywhere in the world. This was the era of the Celtic Tiger when economists and international bodies lauded the "Irish Miracle" and held the Irish State up as a model for others to follow. Today it lies in ruins, the gains of the past several years erased almost overnight.

The collapse of the economy has been dramatic, after a long boom, and after growing by six per cent in 2007, Ireland was the first economy in the European Union to enter recession in 2008.[3] The economy shrank by 7.5 per cent in the last three months of 2008 and in the whole of 2008 shrank by 2.3 per

---

2 Quoted in Ireland's unemployment rises to 11.4 per cent, Guardian, 29/04/09.
3 Irish Economy in Recession, Economics Help Blog, 26/06/09.

cent, the first decline since 1983. The decline accelerated in the first quarter of 2009 with Gross Domestic Product (GDP) down 8.5 per cent from the same quarter in the previous year, and Gross National Product (GNP) down 12 per cent.[4] According to an International Monetary Fund (IMF) report, the stress on the economy exceeded "that being faced currently by any other advanced economy and matches episodes of the most severe economic distress in post–World War II history." The IMF forecast that Ireland's economy would contract by 13.5 per cent between 2008 and 2010, and start to grow around one per cent in 2011 before it stabilizes around 2.5 per cent for several years.[5] The Economic and Social Research Institute estimated that the total decline in output would be just under 12 per cent to the end of 2010, a sharper decline than in any industrialised country since the Great Depression.[6] Over a two–year period, from the crest of growth to the trough of contraction when this book is written, there has been a decline of almost 20 per cent.

The economic crisis has manifested itself in falling investment and rapidly rising unemployment. From its peak level at the beginning of 2007, gross fixed capital formation fell by 42.6 per cent (€6.1 billion in monetary terms). This is nearly three times as great as the decline in investment in the United Kingdom (UK) and United States (US), and almost four times that of Germany. You have to look to the US between 1929–31 for a decline in investment of similar magnitude.[7] The impact of the economic collapse on employment has been devastating. Unemployment doubled from under six per cent to over 12.6 per cent at the beginning of 2010.[8] The ESRI predicted a further 76,000 job losses in 2010, with unemployment pushing towards 14 per cent.[9] The rise in unemployment has fallen hardest on the young. The Irish State now has the 2nd highest youth unemployment in Western Europe, with a quarter of

---

4 Quarterly National Accounts Quarter 1 2009, Central Statistics Office, June 2009.

5 Irish economy is the sickest of them all, IMF study claims, Daily Telegraph, 25/06/09.

6 Quarterly Economic Commentary, ESRI, Spring 2009.

7 Ireland – The nature of the crisis, Socialist Economic Bulletin, 09/10/09.

8 The Truth about the Recession, People Before Profit, 04/01/10.

9 Quarterly Economic Commentary, ESRI, Winter 2009.

young men aged between 18 and 24 out of work.[10] These figures would be even worse had Ireland not experienced a net outward migration of 40,000 in the same period.[11] The return of emigration, which had been a blight for so many decades and which many would have assumed belonged to the past, is a stark illustration of the severity of the crisis.

The nature of the crisis

This crisis has three distinct but related elements, a general decline of the economy manifested in negative GDP growth, falling investment and rising unemployment; a financial crisis, particularly within the banking sector, and a deterioration of public finances. Although the elements overlap, it was the financial crisis that triggered the most rapid economic decline and deteriorating public finances, even while it in turn was due to excessive concentration on the construction sector in the 'real' economy. While this had been building for some time, when it finally broke in 2008 its impact was dramatic and rapid. Throughout that year the stresses and strains upon Irish banks grew as they revealed that they had lost money in bad loans and were struggling to repair their balance sheets. At the same time the Government and financial regulator, not to mention the banks themselves, assured everyone that the banks were fundamentally sound. Nevertheless share prices collapsed as investors and money markets withdrew support. All this came to a head in late September 2008 with a run in the wholesale markets on the joint–second largest Irish bank, Anglo Irish.[12] A large section of Ireland's financial sector was on the brink of bankruptcy, and would have failed completely without state intervention. This intervention staved off the banks' immediate collapse but left them in a zombie state facing huge losses equivalent to about 20 per cent of GDP.[13]

The collapse of public finances also occurred very rapidly. In 2006, the General Government Surplus was three per cent of

---

10 Youth Council opposed to youth unemployment payment cuts, National Youth Council of Ireland, 30/11/09.

11 Quarterly Economic Commentary, ESRI, Winter 2009.

12 Morgan Kelly – The Irish Credit Bubble – WP09/32, UCD Centre for Economic Research, December 2009.

13 Irish economy is the sickest of them all, IMF study claims, Daily Telegraph, 25/06/09.

GDP but the contraction of consumption and employment (leading to higher social security costs and a slump in tax revenues), brought about a complete reversal so that the deficit reached almost 12 per cent of GDP in 2009. The level of national debt may have exceeded 41 per cent of GDP in 2009, up from 12 per cent in 2007.[14] The State was on course for a deficit of close to €30 billion. For every €1 it was spending, it was taking in only 50 cents in taxation.[15] Even after three cost cutting budgets within one year the deficit continued to grow and the Irish State developed one of the highest budget deficits in the European Union and far above the EU rules of three per cent.[16]

The economic collapse has been presented, not least by the Government, as a consequence of the international financial crisis. The opposition parties, on the other hand, have pointed to its home grown nature (evidenced by its relative severity within Ireland) in an attempt to saddle the governing parties with the blame. While it is wrong to simply blame the global financial meltdown for the Irish collapse the same forces that created the former produced the latter. If the crisis has proved more severe here than elsewhere this reflects both the underlying weakness of the Irish economy and the consequent impact of regulatory failure. While there are some parallels with other parts of the world, such as the US, the crisis in Ireland has its own particular features and dynamic so that, for example, while exotic financial products did not feature so prominently there was no shortage of similar wild and excessive speculation on real estate. If there has been one thing that has marked out the Irish economy in recent years it is the expansion of bank lending and the dramatic growth of the property market. The nexus between finance and property, and the credit fuelled growth it produced, has therefore been central to the unfolding crisis.

Over a period of eight years the Irish economy became a highly geared bet on the profits to be made by building tens of

---

14 Quarterly Economic Commentary, ESRI, Winter 2009.
15 Nama set to shift wealth to lenders and developers, Irish Times, 26/08/09.
16 The Truth about the Recession, People Before Profit, 04/01/10.

thousands of houses and offices. From 2004 to 2008, banks threw money at housing, with almost €50 billion advanced in mortgages. The banks threw billions at property developers who were desperate to acquire land banks and to fund the building of new housing estates.[17] The level of house building reached unprecedented levels with around 90,000 houses built in 2006, compared to 200,000 in the UK, which has fifteen times the population. The Irish State became the largest house builder per head of population in the EU. According to the standards of the Organisation for Economic Coordination and Development (OECD), a body of the most developed states, housing starts were 26 per cent above sustainable levels.[18]

The accelerating growth of the property sector was not a reflection of growing commercial or residential demand but of speculative investment, the motor for which was the expansion of bank lending. Irish bank lending (mostly developer loans and mortgages) grew almost seven–fold to €400 billion in the ten years after the Irish State joined the euro at the beginning of 1999.[19] By mid–2005 annual credit growth in the Eurozone was just over seven per cent while in Ireland it was heading for 30 per cent.[20] In 2008 it reached 200 per cent of national income.[21]

Given Ireland's relative underdevelopment and lack of historically accumulated wealth this rapid rise in speculative lending had to be financed by foreign borrowing. The expansion of the financial and property sectors was therefore accompanied by a build up of foreign indebtedness. Irish banks' borrowing from abroad to lend to Irish residents soared from 10 to 41 per cent of GDP between 2003 and 2005.[22] By the end of the first quarter of 2009, gross external debt amounted to €1,693 billion.[23] The expansion of lending had the effect of dramatically ramping up property prices and between 2000 and

17 How Ireland's economy went from boom to bust, Management Today, 01/06/09.

18 Irish Economy: Riding For A Fall?, Daily Reckoning, 13/08/07.

19 Rogue banks cost us all a fortune. So who was protecting them?, Herald, 22/12/09.

20 Greatest Bubble in History: Warnings ignored in US and Ireland, Finfacts, 02/11/08.

21 Kelly, December 2009.

22 Greatest Bubble in History: Warnings ignored in US and Ireland, Finfacts, 02/11/08.

23 Quarterly external debt report, Central Statistics Office, 30/06/09.

2006 house prices doubled relative to income and rents.[24] At their peak prices were around four times higher in real terms than in 1995.[25] During this period the whole economy became increasingly dependent on property. From accounting for four to six per cent of national income in the 1990s, the usual level for a developed economy, house building grew to 15 per cent at the peak of the bubble in 2006–07, with another six per cent coming from other construction.[26] Direct employment in construction rose from 126,000 in early 1998 to 282,000 in December 2006[27], accounting for 13 per cent of the total workforce and more than 17 per cent of the private non–farm workforce. (The corresponding proportions for the UK and US were 7 per cent and 5.4 per cent respectively.)[28] Public finances also became reliant on this sector with property related taxes accounting for 17 per cent of total government revenue,[29] up from 4 per cent in 1995. In November 2004, the then Finance Minister Brian Cowen, disclosed that the State collected 28 per cent of the cost of each new housing unit in taxes and public charges.[30]

Thus while the economy appeared to be booming it was also sowing the seeds of its own destruction, for this boom could only be sustained by generating massive amounts of credit and a huge increase in debt. Such speculative growth has an inevitable limit, as the creation of debt cannot continue without creation of real incomes and wealth to pay it all back. A point is reached when borrowers become reluctant to take on what appears as impossibly large levels of debt. When this happens the upward spiral of borrowing and prices starts to work in reverse. The peaking of the average size of mortgages approved occurred in the third quarter of 2006 and was an indicator that Ireland had reached a tipping point. By the middle of 2007 the construction industry was in decline as unsold units began to

24 Best to ignore the cheerleaders for the property sector, Southern Star, 31/12/09.

25 Economic Survey of Ireland, OECD, November 2009.

26 Kelly, December 2009.

27 Greatest Bubble in History: Warnings ignored in US and Ireland, Finfacts, 02/11/08.

28 Ireland's Celtic Tiger 2005: Built to last or on a foundation of quicksand?, Finfacts, 06/12/05.

29 Irish Economy: Riding For A Fall?, Daily Reckoning, 13/08/07.

30 Irish Economy: State bank guarantee tolls the death knell of the Celtic Tiger, Finfacts, 04/10/08.

accumulate.[31] There was a 24 per cent fall in output in the sector, the biggest fall on record, and fully 15 per cent of Irish property was lying empty. [32] Prices stopped increasing and when they did many speculators were left with property they could not afford but could not afford to sell. Massive oversupply led to falling prices and huge amounts of money lent by banks to property developers becoming bad debts. This in turn led to the banking crisis and the crisis in State finances.

In this sequence of events it is the bursting of the housing bubble that has brought about the ruinous situation for Ireland's economy, banks and public finances. It also has to be emphasised that the onset of the Irish crisis predates the global financial crash. For example, the Irish property market peaked in 2006, more than a year before the U.S. subprime mortgage mess.[33] So while there are obvious parallels, and while the international credit crunch and recession certainly made the situation worse, the Irish State's economic collapse is not merely a consequence of the global meltdown but is a homemade crisis with its own internal dynamic.

This dynamic is similar to that in the US and other countries but what we have said so far is a story, not an explanation. How could property development continue way beyond what could conceivably be usefully occupied, either as residential accommodation or as offices and productive enterprise? At the very least it is obviously and undeniably true that the economic system, geared to profit and not social need, not only made such a crisis possible but, as most of the rest of the world testifies, almost inevitable.

Political corruption and regulatory failure are certainly part of the explanation but these too are not accidental but also the result of a system whose dynamic is unplanned and atomized pursuit of the private accumulation of profit. Given such imperatives the political and regulatory regime had a clear role to facilitate this, which it did in Ireland just as it did in the US,

---

31 Kelly, December 2009.
32 Record decline hits Irish economy, BBC News, 26/03/09.
33 The fall of the Celtic Tiger, Globe and Mail, 28/11/08.

UK and in many other states. The possibility of a bubble was well known to political leaders, financiers and regulators, at least in the US, but it was considered easier to make money during the boom and clear up after a mess created by the bubble bursting than to stop it inflating in the first place. So far this has been the strategy adopted, with the mass of ordinary people paying for the rampant speculation of the bankers and developers. In the US and UK there is much concern that this has now created an incentive for creation of future bubbles since the tab has been picked up by working class and middle class taxpayers, and that those profiting from future bubbles may expect similar rescues. In Ireland the weakness of the economic fundamentals makes such a prospect somewhat more distant but also potentially more lethal. Rising world interest rates and/or another recession would be devastating. For what the crisis has exposed is the hollow and fragile character of the much lauded Celtic Tiger economy.

Turning point

While the Celtic Tiger phenomenon may be defined as the long period of economic growth from the early 1990s to 2008, there are important discontinuities within it. From this perspective, the Celtic Tiger had two distinct phases – an earlier phase that was driven by foreign investment in production, and a later phase (which we have outlined above) driven by credit–fuelled property speculation. The turning point may be traced to 2001. In this year, the Irish economy was caught in a minor US recession, investment driven growth peaked and capital began to flow elsewhere.[34] GDP growth slowed to just two per cent, a fall so sharp that it briefly felt like a recession.[35] What followed was a boom of a different kind as money poured into commercial and residential property. This was encouraged by low interest rates and government tax measures that made investment in property particularly attractive. Property tax incentives that invited high earners to invest in property, and write off their value over a seven–year period against income,

---

34 How deep is the Irish economic crisis? SWP, 02/04/09.

35 How Ireland's economy went from boom to bust, Management Today, 01/06/09.

had been introduced in the 1980s and were now extended in scope. Capital gains tax was cut from 40 per cent to 20 per cent, which made investment in property compelling for high earners who were paying a top tax rate of over 40 per cent. Banks introduced five–year interest only loans and the European Central Bank cut its benchmark rate to two per cent in mid–2003.[36] To a significant degree this new boom, which ultimately proved so disastrous, was consciously engineered as a replacement for what had gone before.

A number of explanations have been put forward for the emergence of the Celtic Tiger. One is that the Irish economy experienced a delayed catch–up with the rest of Western Europe. Once policies of national self–sufficiency had been abandoned and those of fiscal rectitude plus others were implemented the economy could experience the growth that was always possible. The theoretical perspective informing this is that creating an environment for free market forces allowed them to combine to produce the growth that occurred over the 1990s and to a lesser extent in the noughties. In this sense there was a certain amount of inevitability about such a process once the right policy choices by the Irish State were adopted.[37]

A second part of this explanation is that policies of low taxation, an educated and English–speaking workforce, a business friendly environment and helpful Irish State attracted the foreign direct investment that created the Celtic Tiger. There are differences among academics over the relative importance of the various elements of this explanation but one objection is applicable to all. The Irish State has pursued a policy of opening up to the world economy since at least the late 1950s. It has also offered tax incentives, a business–friendly political and social environment and an educated workforce since the 1960s. Yet only in the 1990s did the economy 'take off'. In fact in the 1980s the economy of the Irish State was in a mess, with most of the factors that supposedly led to success in place, but accompanied by massive unemployment, massive emigration

---

36 Irish Economy: State bank guarantee tolls the death knell of the Celtic Tiger, Finfacts, 04/10/08.

37 Patrick Honohan – Ireland's economic miracle: A story of delayed catch–up, TCD, 2007.

and a huge national debt. It is not credible to argue that the growth of the 1990s and after was in any sense inevitable.

It is quite clear that foreign direct investment by primarily US multinationals was the dynamic motor of the Celtic Tiger boom. Decisions to invest in Ireland as opposed to anywhere else are obviously ones that require a global perspective. It is developments at the global level that must provide the starting point for any explanation of the development of the Irish economy.

The emergence of the Celtic Tiger was bound up with a new phase of growth of the world economy over the last 20 or so years. On the basis of increased levels of labour exploitation; increased availability of cheapened capital and new markets and sources of supply, not least in Eastern Europe and the former Soviet Union; plus the application of new computer based technology, capitalism was able once again to increase profitability. This process, often described as globalisation, witnessed renewed growth of a financial sector that disciplined industrial capital and taxed the working class through expansion of debt, assisting the more rapid shifting of capital to more profitable locations. In this period there was worldwide growth of foreign investment especially marked in information and communication technology. The Irish State benefited from this globalisation and the processes associated with it. This included the development of the EU with its transfer of subsidies to offset increased competition with domestic capital, and the wave of inward foreign direct investment which moved to take advantage of the inauguration of the Single European Market in 1992.

A key moment came in 1989 with Dell establishing a plant in Limerick and Intel setting up an operation in Leixlip on the outskirts of Dublin, which at its height would employ 5,000 people.[38] Over the next few years these were followed by a range of other multinational firms, including Gateway, AST, Apple, Hewlett–Packard, Siemens–Nixdorf, Fujitsu, Microsoft

---

38 How Ireland's economy went from boom to bust, Management Today, 01/06/09.

and Oracle. Ireland witnessed a massive year–on–year growth of foreign direct investment (FDI), going from $85.1 million in 1989 to $25,501 million ($25.5 billion) in 2000. For a number of years the Irish State, with only one per cent of Europe's population, attracted up to 25 per cent of all US greenfield investment in Europe.[39] One of the consequences of such investment was a surge in exports. Between 1990 and 1999 the value of 'Irish' exports grew from £14.3 billion to £52.2 billion. The largest increases were in organic chemicals, computer equipment and electrical machinery. Foreign owned companies produced 65 per cent of gross output and exported on average 89 per cent of what they produced, rising to 95 per cent for US–owned companies. They came to dominate the manufacturing sector in Ireland, accounting for more than 50 per cent of output compared to an average of 19 per cent for other EU countries.[40]

The influx of foreign investment had a dramatic affect on economic growth and the size of the labour force. Between 1993 and 1998 GDP increased by 45 per cent with annual rates of growth approaching 10 per cent while unemployment tumbled.[41] Between 1989 and 1997, net new jobs increased by 23 per cent or 248,500. The numbers at work increased from 1.09 million in 1989 to 1.22 million in 1994; to 1.34 million in 1997 and 1.67 million by 2000. The growth in the labour force was particularly large between 1997 and 2000, and reduced unemployment qualitatively from a high of 10.3 per cent in 1997 to a low rate of 4 per cent in 2000.[42] Labour force participation rates rose from 53.9 per cent in 1983 to 65 per cent in 2003[43] and immigration increased. Ireland was transformed into being a country of immigration after a century and a half of continuous emigration and these trends continued into the second phase of economic growth. Over the whole growth period employment in the Irish State increased by 75 per cent,

39 Irish Economy: State bank guarantee tolls the death knell of the Celtic Tiger, Finfacts, 04/10/08.

40 The endangered Celtic tiger, Socialism Today, February 2008.

41 How Ireland's economy went from boom to bust, Management Today, 01/06/09.

42 The endangered Celtic tiger, Socialism Today, February 2008.

43 U. Becker and H. Schwartz (eds) Employment 'Miracles' in Critical Comparison, Amsterdam, VU University Press, 2005, p.12.

rising from 1.2 million in 1990 to 2.1 million in 2007. The rate of unemployment dropped to historically low levels, averaging 4.5 per cent in 2007. In this year a net inward migration of over 67,000 was recorded.[44]

Economic growth and the accompanying expansion of employment served to raise the level of prosperity in Ireland. It is estimated that average living standards rose by one–half.[45] Even though the benefits of growth flowed disproportionably to the capitalist class, with the share of national income going to wages actually falling (from 71.2 to 54 per cent)[46], workers did experience a real uplift. For example, between 1989 and 1999, there was an average increase in take–home pay of 35 per cent, two thirds from pay rises and the rest from tax cuts.[47] A significant section of the Irish labour force was now involved in advanced manufacturing production, in sectors associated with higher than average profits. Workers therefore had the potential to win gains for themselves and set a benchmark for those in other sectors, but this potential was never fully realised. Such gains that were made had more to do with the natural propensity of a tight labour market to raise wages in a period of boom than any application of collective power by a strong and assertive labour movement.

Weak foundations

There is an assumption that if Ireland had kept to the path of foreign investment and export led growth the current economic catastrophe could have been avoided; but this model of growth had its inherent weaknesses and limitations. The forces that were driving it were essentially temporary in character. The influx of capital in the early 90s was a consequence of a new phase of capitalist global expansion and not only was there was no guarantee that this would continue, but even if it did, no guarantee that Ireland would remain a favoured site for foreign

44 Quarterly Economic Commentary, ESRI, Winter 2009.

45 Irish Economy: State bank guarantee tolls the death knell of the Celtic Tiger, Finfacts, 04/10/08.

46 Ireland: government nationalises Anglo Irish Bank while the country faces the second worst recession in the EU, In Defence of Marxism, 28/01/09.

47 The endangered Celtic tiger, Socialism Today, February 2008.

capital investment. The mobile nature of such capital meant that it could easily transfer to other countries if there were even higher profits to be gained elsewhere, and as the decade progressed Ireland found itself competing with China and Eastern Europe as a site for investment. Its small size meant that a relatively small share of internationally mobile investment could make a large difference to the country but the movement of supply and demand in the capitalist market also meant that this could hardly fail to be reflected in rising wages, which gradually undercut the attractiveness of the State to foreign investment faced with alternative and cheaper locations. Tax cuts and rising debt were both mechanisms used maximally to offset this and only socially repressive measures in the end could have suppressed wages sufficiently to offset increased demand for labour and this too would have had only a temporary effect, never mind the political difficulties involved.

As it turned out the early phase of the Celtic Tiger didn't survive the first shock to globalisation, falling victim to the minor recession that hit the US in 2001. After this capital began to flow elsewhere. In the four years after 2000, the rate of foreign investment in Ireland stopped growing. In two years it was similar to the figure for 2000, but in the other two it was way down (2001 – $9,572m, 2002 – $29,131m, 2003 – $26,599m, 2004 – $9,100m).[48] The sectoral composition of investment also shifted with an increasing portion going into finance and services. US capital was withdrawing from manufacturing and as a proportion of the economy it began to contract. Irish full–time employment in manufacturing and internationally traded services fell 10,297 from 315,418 in 2000 to 305,121 in 2007.[49] By the time the crisis erupted only 13 per cent of the Irish workforce was employed in this sector.[50]

The 2001 shock marked a shift of the Irish economy towards credit driven growth. However, it would wrong to disconnect the earlier period of "good" growth from the "bad" that followed, or to put the transition from one to the other down to

---

48 The endangered Celtic tiger, Socialism Today, February 2008.

49 Irish General Election 2007: Plan for 250,000 new jobs but don't ask for specifics, Finfacts, 26/04/07.

50 How deep is the Irish economic crisis? SWP, 02/04/09.

subjective factors such as poor decisions at Government level. The reality was that by 2001 the economic boom, based on foreign investment and exports, was faltering. Its failure brought the new credit fuelled boom into being and ultimately led to the dramatic collapse of the Irish economy. That this was no peculiar Irish phenomenon is proved by the explosion of credit across many of the most developed states.

What has been a particular feature of the Irish economy despite, in part because of, the boom is continued relative underdevelopment. Despite enjoying a long period of growth, and attracting investment from companies in the most advanced sectors of the world economy, the Irish State continues to lag behind in many areas. A striking example of this is the slow pace of broadband development. In 2008, a survey found that over half of Irish people had never used the internet.[51] The boom did not change the relative weakness of native industrial capital. Despite unprecedented conditions for growth the indigenous sector had not developed the power to drive economic growth in the absence of foreign investment. To this extent the Irish State remains one dominated by the capital accumulation needs of foreign capital. The wide gap (20 per cent) between GDP and GNP[52] illustrates the degree to which value is leaving the country. This combined with political weakness constitutes continuing imperialist domination. It also demonstrates the impossibility of any meaningful 'independent' development. The Bank of Ireland reported in December 2005 that only three per cent of Irish small and medium enterprises (SMEs) are of medium size with more than 50 employees. Overseas expansion and exporting are dependant on businesses growing to a medium size, yet the bank's research indicated that only seven per cent of Irish SMEs intended to expand abroad in 2006. This contrasts sharply with the UK where medium enterprises, which employ 30 per cent of the workforce, are an important driver of the economy.[53] No Irish high–tech

51 Irish Economy: State bank guarantee tolls the death knell of the Celtic Tiger, Finfacts, 04/10/08.

52 Is Ireland really the second wealthiest nation in the world? New Economist Blog, 09/09/05.

53 Bank of Ireland says only 3 per cent of Irish SMEs have more than 50 employees, Finfacts, 05/12/05.

company has revenue of over $100m and the largest, Iona Technologies, was sold to a US firm in 2008.[54]

If a strong indigenous capitalism capable of intersecting with world imperialism on an even minimally equal basis has not been created by the economic boom of the past fifteen or so years it is very unlikely to ever develop. The relative weakness of Irish capital in the most productive sectors of the economy has made the indigenous capitalist class more dependent on parasitical activities. That is why the 'gombeen man' has played such a role in our history and continues to do so today. Since 2001 about €60 billion (equity and borrowings) was invested by the Irish in commercial property. In the same period less than €1.5 billion in venture capital flowed to Irish–owned companies.[55] The windfalls from the property boom were invested in overseas commercial property. In 2007, €13.9 billion was invested into European property deals by Irish capitalists while they couldn't even raise €200 million for venture capital projects.[56]

In February 2010, a report from Davy Research declared that the "years of high income [were] largely wasted." "The unproductive capital stock exceeded the productive stock by €14 billion [in 2000]. By 2008, that gap was a whopping €118 billion." Much of this productive stock was in the import intensive areas of retail, transport and storage, was mainly foreign owned, not technologically advanced and beset by surplus capacity. "Most of the rest of the increase in our 'core' productive capital stock was related to the state or semi–state sectors. It was not driven by private enterprise. . . . The problem with the glut of investment in the wrong places is that our technological capacity has not advanced much over the last decade.'[57] In other words the free market system had built hundreds of thousands of houses which no one wanted to live in or could not afford; created an economic and financial disaster

---

54 Iona Technologies sold to US software group in $162m deal, Irish Times, 26/06/08.

55 Irish Economy: State bank guarantee tolls the death knell of the Celtic Tiger, Finfacts, 04/10/08.

56 Irish investors were the second biggest net investors in commercial property across Europe in 2007, Finfacts, 03/03/10.

57 Davy Research Report: Irish Economy February 19 2010.

and, even during the boom, created little of lasting value. Instead it left a legacy of unemployment and a level of debt that will weigh down generations. And this is the system that virtually every politician and expert commentator says we must rely on to get us out of the current mess. A mess only possible because of the blind faith placed in it in the first place. It should therefore come as no surprise that the interests of the small elite who benefited from the system are now the centre of concern of the policies to chart an economic recovery.

This strategy, being pushed by Government and employers, has three main elements. A bailout of the financial system, which it is claimed will get credit flowing again; cuts in public spending, which it is claimed will stabilise public finances; and reductions in workers wages and conditions, which it is claimed will allow Ireland Inc. to regain lost competitiveness. The stated objective is to put the country in a position to take advantage of the undoubted upturn in the global economy.

NAMA

In late 2008 a large section of the financial sector was on the brink of bankruptcy. In response the Government made a number of interventions – these included the beggar–thy–neighbour policy of the 100 per cent liabilities guarantee, claimed at the time to be the cheapest rescue of a finance system in the world; a round of recapitalisation which injected over €10 billion into the system;[58] and the nationalisation of Anglo Irish Bank. It was on the back of the failure of these measures that the idea of the establishment of a state run 'bad bank', which would take on the toxic assets held by the commercial banks, started to gain currency.

In February 2009, the Government–appointed economist Peter Bacon, himself an associate of developers, to assess the possibility of creating a "bad bank" or risk insurance scheme.[59] Acting on his report the Government began preparations to

---

58 Government looking for a 'blank cheque' from taxpayers, Irish Times, 31/07/09.
59 State hires Bacon for 'bad bank' role, Irish Times, 20/02/09.

establish a bad loans agency to cleanse the banks of their toxic assets.[60] This took a more concrete form in August 2009 with the publication of the draft legislation to establish NAMA, the National Asset Management Agency. Its proposal to create a 'bad bank' envisaged the Government purchasing loans with a face value of up to €90 billion from the banks.[61] The new agency would take control of the loans and the properties which had been pledged as security against the loans, holding them until the market improved whereupon they could be sold and the money invested recouped. The transfer of assets to NAMA would be achieved through the issuing of Government bonds that would be used to acquire property loans from the banks at a discounted rate. The banks could then cash the bonds with the European Central Bank. The claim made for this process was that it would restore the liquidity of the banks, enabling them to start lending again and thereby hasten the pace of recovery.

Confirmation that NAMA would be a mechanism to bail out the banks came on September 16 when the Finance Minister announced how much it would be paying to transfer the loans to the new agency. These figures came during the opening of the Dail debate on the legislation that would pave the way for its creation. The Finance Minister announced that NAMA would take €77 billion worth of loans off the banks, with the State paying around €54 billion for these – a discount of around 30 per cent. His department estimated that the current value of these properties, if they were to be put on the market, would be in the region of €47 billion – a write–down of 47 per cent.[62] It estimated that, in the long term – in other words, in about seven to ten years, it was reasonable to expect that they might be worth €54 billion, the so–called long–term economic value of the assets. In fact the Government were concealing the true costs of NAMA by making a number of unfounded assumptions and engaging in a financial sleight of hand. The most blatant was to deliberately underestimate the fall in the value of the assets underpinning the loans that would be taken into the bad

60 Annus horribilis for Irish banks, Irish Times, 31/12/09.

61 Taxpayers can't lumped with shareholders win, Herald, 31/07/09.

62 Nama smoke begins to clear, Sunday Business Post, 20/09/09.

bank. Various transactions and court cases had provided evidence that there had been at least a 60 per cent fall from peak for land and development projects and a 47 per cent fall for other property based assets. This would leave the current market value of the NAMA assets at €39 billion, not the €47 billion claimed by the Government. On these estimates the gap between what would be paid for the assets and what they were worth would be €15 billion.[63]

The second hidden cost lay in the mechanism used to finance NAMA. The Government would exchange bonds for the loans and the banks could then cash these bonds with the European Central Bank. This however was not free money, despite absurd claims to the contrary from some members of the Government. The State would have to pay interest on these bonds, or rather the tax payer would. NAMA bonds would have an interest rate set at a half percent above the ECB's main refinancing rate. While the ECB rate was currently one percent it was expected to go in only one direction. The amount of interest paid on NAMA bonds could increase significantly as interest rates on the bonds rose.[64] This would not be matched by interest receipts from the loans taken over because it was claimed that only 40 per cent of these were cash generating.

The third concealed cost of NAMA was to be a further round of recapitalisation of the banks.[65] It may have thrown people a little than the Government left some of the toxic loans on the books of the banks rather than taking the full €90 billion worth into NAMA but this was really a sleight of hand designed to bring down the headline total. In the case of the nationalised Anglo–Irish the public had already taken on its full loan book. It was hoped that NAMA moving into operation would be the trigger for the banks to declare losses on the bad loans left on their books and appeal for new capital. AIB had already said that it needed €2 billion in new capital.[66] It was estimated that Anglo Irish needed an additional €4 billion in fresh capital to

---

63 Do the Nama property sums add up?, Sunday Business Post, 20/09/09.

64 NAMA bond yield formula finally revealed, Irish Economy Blog, 17/09/09.

65 Ryan predicts increased State ownership of banks, Irish Times, 19/09/09.

66 Nama smoke begins to clear, Sunday Business Post, 20/09/09.

continue to operate. This might rise to €6 billion or more due to further write–downs on loans not transferred.[67] Despite the deliberately misleading way the costs of NAMA were calculated and presented there was no hiding the fact that it was a bailout for the banks.

At the end of March 2010, sceptics of the Government's claims were confirmed in their views when the Government revealed the discounts necessary on the first tranche of loans to leave the distressed banks and be taken on by NAMA. The scale of the discounts revealed somewhat more accurately the scale of the reckless lending. Finance Minister Brian Lenihan had to acknowledge that "our worst fears have been surpassed".[68] The Government had promoted NAMA as a once and for all solution for the Irish banking system. It had trumpeted it as the solution in direct opposition to state ownership, even while it nationalised Anglo–Irish. Yet the transfer of the first loans in 2010 made clear what was long obvious – that NAMA was not an alternative to state ownership but a prelude to it. Richard Bruton of Fine Gael called the bail out instituted by NAMA 'socialism for bankers' but massive corporate welfare was obviously not any sort of socialism, which is predicated on workers ownership and control. The Bruton remark was one of many reflecting shock at the cost of the bailout. The toxic nature of the loans taken on by NAMA was revealed in the extent of discounts applied to the face value of the loans. Instead of a predicted 30 per cent, discounts ranged from 58 per cent on those taken from the Irish Nationwide Building Society and 50 per cent at Anglo Irish to 35 per cent at Bank of Ireland. Some loans examined were given a value of zero by NAMA. The security on the loans taken by the banks in many cases simply didn't exist. Time, perhaps, to recall that the directors of the banks had received huge bonuses based on arguments about the need to attract and retain skills and talent. It was estimated that the five institutions covered by NAMA needed to boost their reserves by €21.8 billion with Anglo Irish possibly requiring a further €10 billion, and this on top of the

---

67 State faces new Anglo cash call, Sunday Business Post, 20/09/09.
68 Nama banking revelations shocking, says Lenihan, Irish Times, 21/03/10.

€11 billion already pumped into them.[69] The final bill for bailing out the banks was now estimated to be €82,875,000,000.[70]

The announcement of the amount required by the banks came at the same time as reports revealed greater and greater falls in bank lending and increases in interest charged on mortgages. Working people, as taxpayers, were to almost entirely foot the bill for recapitalisation while as customers they were to pay again by making the financial institutions profitable on a recurring basis.

The Government based its strategy on the argument that the international financial institutions would punish the state for letting one of its banks go bust while some more independent economists wondered whether in fact some might regard the Irish as crazy for pumping billions into zombie banks. In any case the weight of assertion from economic commentators employed currently or previously by financial institutions; from the experts of international financial institutions themselves saved from their own profligacy and with possibly their own money invested in Irish banks; from the IMF which specialises in bailing out insolvent countries by lending them money so that they can in fact repay the banks; from the EU which represented the European interests of the same banks looking to save their misguided investments, and of course the credit rating agencies which had given sub–prime mortgage backed securities AAA ratings; all these backed the Government. Of course what made the veiled threats of all these actors credible was that states all round the world had bailed them out. In effect working class taxpayers were bailing out an international financial system which threatened not to loan their states money if they didn't do it. At the end of the day the Government was hoping that by getting the majority to pay to save the banks it could at some point turn round and claimed that it had been proved correct because workers had indeed paid to save them.

---

69 'Horrifying' understates dire plight of Irish banks, Irish Times, 21/03/10.

70 Is your head spinning from bank numbers? Let's try again, Irish Times, 03/04/10.

Budget Cuts

While Governments may deny it, and have constructed various accounting tricks to conceal it, the bailouts drained money from public services. In some cases, such as recapitalisation, there is a direct transfer of resources from public services into the financial system. For example, the €4 billion initially injected into Anglo Irish Bank corresponds to the €4 billion of cuts introduced in the December 2009 budget. It is not just that the two sums are the same; it's that they come from the same source. The money used to fund public services, including the wages and pensions of those who work in them, and the money used to fund the banks is drawn from the general public spending pot made up of tax revenues and increasingly from borrowing. The more that the Government borrows to fund the bailout, the more it needs to demonstrate to international financial markets that its debts can be repaid. This means that it has to bear down ever harder on public spending. It is a case of the working class being made to pay for the crisis, and of resources being moved from labour to capital.

The recession will end at some point. This is the way capitalist economies work, with downturns recreating the basis for future upturns which then prepare the ground for a future downturn. The financial crisis will be resolved at the expense of the incomes and livelihoods of the working majority unless the latter prevent it. It is the State which is the mechanism to achieve this so that the debts of the bankers become everyone else's debts. This agenda has been articulated most comprehensively in the report of the Special Group on Public Service Numbers and Expenditure Programmes, established by the Government in 2008 to recommend cuts in public spending. Its findings were issued in July 2009.

The body, usually dubbed An Bord Snip Nua, gives a clear indication of the huge attack that has been launched on working people. It sets out a comprehensive programme for the dismantling of public services and the reduction of wages and conditions across the board. Though nominally independent, the Special Group, in terms of its remit of identifying savings in public spending, and of its membership drawn from finance and academia, was fixed to produce a report that fitted with the objectives of the Government. Its purpose was to give a pseudo intellectual gloss to some of the measures that the Government wanted to introduce in future budgets.

The Group's nominal independence also allowed the governing parties to distance themselves from its most unpopular proposals while it worked steadily to implement them. Thus everyone was told that nothing had been decided, and the report produced by An Bord Snip Nua was merely a 'menu' of options. This menu proposed some €5.3 billion worth of spending cuts over a two–year period ending in 2011.[71] The areas targeted for the deepest cuts were health, education and social security. It proposed 17,000 job losses across the public service, the bulk of these going in education (7,000) and health (6,000).[72] It also proposed an increase in the number and level of user charges for public services. This came alongside a proposal for a five per cent across the board reduction in welfare payments[73] and reductions in the wages and terms and conditions of public servants. It was a triple whammy of job cuts, reduced wages and higher charges – a combination that would significantly reduce living standards.

Already under strain from years of underfunding, the proposals would mean one of the highest pupil to teacher ratios in the EU. Measures included the closure of rural schools, longer working hours for teachers, outsourcing and rationalisation. All this would translate into a 7.3 per cent cut in the numbers working in education and overall annual cuts of €746m to the education budget – a 7.9 percent reduction in the 2009 estimated spend for the sector. Primary schools would take the brunt of the cuts, with the recommendation to axe 2,000 of 10,500 special needs assistants, reduce English language support and increase class sizes.[74] Given that many primary schools are being propped up

71 Economic Shock Therapy – Irish Style, Socialism or Barbarism Blog, 16/07/09.
72 Decision time for Government and unions, Irish Times, 17/07/09.
73 Report seeks €5.3 billion in savings, Irish Times, 17/07/09.
74 Education hit hard with plan to slash 6,900 jobs, Irish Independent, 17/07/09.

and kept going by fundraising and parent contributions the impact of a 20 per cent cut in school funding[75] could be devastating. The closure of schools would also mean an increase in the number of parents having to pay transport fees, which the report said should rise from €138 a year per pupil to €500 and even higher in time.[76] That the Governing parties, economic experts and journalists could then wax lyrical about Government plans to create a 'knowledge economy' just gave the whole proposal an air of absurdity.

The report demanded that over €1.2 billion be cut from the Health Service Executive's budget in one year alone.[77] To achieve such drastic savings it made a number of recommendations. As in education, a big element was cutting jobs and reducing working conditions. It called for staff cuts of six thousand "at a minimum" by the end of the following year. There would be more outsourcing of services and less reliance on permanent and pensionable staff to do certain duties. This represented further privatisation and the creation of a two tier workforce, with contracted workers on poorer pay and conditions. It would not increase efficiency. Alongside reductions in staff and the inevitable deterioration in service, patients would have to pay more for services. The report recommended that people attending accident and emergency without a GP certificate should pay €125 a visit. Medical card holders should pay €5 per prescription, while those on the Drug Payment Scheme should pay €125 a month for medicines. People on the Long–Term Illness Scheme would also face the €5 prescription charge. Thousands of people on low incomes would lose their medical cards under a proposal to lower the qualification threshold. Also axed would be the entitlement to hold onto a medical card for three years if a person got a job after being out of work for 12 months. Workers who paid PRSI and were entitled to some of the costs of attending a dentist or an optician, and money towards the cost of hearing aids, would lose such assistance. Elderly people and people with a disability who availed of home care packages to support them would be

75 An Bord Snip Nua Report Press Release, INTO, 16/07/09.

76 Report seeks €5.3 billion in savings, Irish Times, 17/07/09.

77 Report seeks €5.3 billion in savings, Irish Times, 17/07/09.

means tested for the first time. The report also called for a review of the Hepatitis C/HIV tribunal, which had been set up to compensate people who had received infected blood and blood products.[78]

Previously social security had been one area of spending that the Government had left largely untouched. The An Bord Snip proposals therefore marked a major shift. Its report claimed that there was a "clear case" for a 5 per cent cut in social welfare rates which would account for €850 million a year.[79] It called for a flat–rate €30 cut in child benefit payments, amounting to more than €500 million.[80] Child benefit would be cut by between €30 and €67 per child per month, depending on the number of children. The state paid €166 each for the first two children but this would fall to €136 per child. The third and subsequent children got €203 a month but it was recommended that for these children this be cut by €67 a month.[81]

Older people would also be hit hard by the report's recommendations, including a five per cent cut in state contributory pensions payments, translating into a reduction of €11 a week in a weekly pension of €230. Over a year this would amount to a cost of €600.[82] There was a suggestion that the age at which people could claim a state pension be raised and the report also called for taxation of the household benefits package for older people, in which elderly people get an allowance to pay their electricity and telephone bills and get a TV licence free of charge.[83] Higher contributions would have to be made by those in nursing homes and home care services would be restricted.[84] Other benefits to be cut or made more restrictive included rent supplement, paid to those on social welfare, family income supplement for those on low incomes, illness benefit and disability allowance. The Government was cautioned not to bow

78 Thousands now face losing medical cards, Irish Independent, 17/07/09.

79 Cut of 5 per cent would drop payments to 2008 levels, Irish Times, 17/07/09.

80 Report seeks €5.3 billion in savings, Irish Times, 17/07/09.

81 Families and elderly to bear brunt of swingeing cutbacks, Irish Independent, 17/07/09.

82 Families and elderly to bear brunt of swingeing cutbacks, Irish Independent, 17/07/09.

83 Cut of 5 per cent would drop payments to 2008 levels, Irish Times, 17/07/09.

84 Thousands now face losing medical cards, Irish Independent, 17/07/09.

to pressure to reintroduce the Christmas social welfare bonus which was "no longer affordable."[85]

Other changes promised further cuts in living standards and one of the biggest arose from the proposals on restructuring of local government. The report called for a €100m cut in funding to local authorities and a reduction in their number from 34 to 22. It also called on them to be "self–financing in the long term", meaning that householders would be faced with a raft of new service charges, and suggested the introduction of water charges as a new source of revenue for country and city councils.[86] While much of the An Bord Snip Report put forward proposals to cut what could be termed the 'social wage' i.e. social security and public services, it also targeted the pay of public sector workers. This was not just about lowering the pay bill through redundancies, but also reducing pay levels. The report called on the Government to initiate a benchmarking review of the public sector.[87] Significantly, such a review would have a remit to look at international pay rates and not confine itself to domestic comparisons.[88] Potentially the benchmark for public sector pay could be based on the lowest level within the EU. This really was a race to the bottom.

The proposals in the report, combined with the cuts already announced in recent budgets, represented a massive assault on the living standards of working people. They were being hit by a three–punch combination of job cuts, reduced wages and higher charges. But the punishment didn't end with the measures outlined within it. The stated aim of the Government was to reach a position in 2013 where the budget deficit – the amount it borrows each year – was less than three per cent of GDP. When the financial collapse hit in 2008 it was looking at a deficit for the year of something in the region of 16 per cent of GDP or over €27 billion. The various measures announced, starting with the 2008 cutbacks and including the two subsequent budgets, trimmed this figure to somewhere in the

85 Report seeks €5.3 billion in savings, Irish Times, 17/07/09.

86 Axe 12 councils, end staff perks and charge for water in home, Irish Independent, 17/07/09.

87 New benchmarking round 'must not exclude pay cuts', Irish Times, 17/07/09.

88 The McCarthy era cuts both ways, Sunday Tribune, 19/07/09.

region of 11 per cent or €20.3 billion. The measures in the An Bord Snip report would get this figure back towards single digits but that still required further cuts.[89] The chair of the Special Group, Colm McCarthy, claimed that the measures taken so far, combined with those set out in its report, only took the Government half way towards its objective. He did not of course consider the additional costs that bailing out the banks would incur over many years, if not generations, into the future.

The striking thing about the response to the An Bord Snip report was the degree of unanimity across the main political parties despite the undeniable fact that cuts would further deflate the economy and in doing so inflict further losses on the banks. The governing parties welcomed the report, putting forward the phoney patriotic argument that everyone shared the pain, while stressing that its proposals were a "menu", which meant that they would be selected as political expediency dictated. If anything the opposition parties were more positive, with Fine Gael claiming that it had been putting forward similar proposals for years[90] and Labour saying that the job cuts outlined were achievable.[91] The only variation was their claim that they could implement the cuts in a more humane manner, surgery as opposed to butchery according to Labour leader Eamonn Gilmore.

European Union

EU membership has been widely viewed as the saviour of Ireland, credited with creating the economic boom, cushioning the impact of the recession, and providing the basis for future recovery. This came to the fore during the second Lisbon Treaty referendum when a wide range of opinion, including that of trade union leaders, political parties and business organisations, mobilised to press for a yes vote. Slogans such as "Vote Yes for Recovery" and "Vote Yes for Jobs" encapsulated the argument that the EU was essential for the Irish State. A

---

89 Decision time for Government and unions, Irish Times, 17/07/09.

90 Report seeks €5.3 billion in savings, Irish Times, 17/07/09.

91 Big job cuts in public service are 'doable' – Gilmore, Irish Times, 18/07/09.

banner held up during one protest in 2008 rather simply demolished all this by asking 'Can we have the Lisbon jobs now please!'

The Irish State has been a member of the EU since 1973, and for most of that period the experience has been a disappointment. In the early years of membership Ireland lost much of its indigenous industry. Low growth, high unemployment and emigration persisted throughout the 1970s and 1980s and only the more recent period of rapid economic growth could produce a more positive view.[92] Yet as we have shown earlier, this growth, certainly in its early phase, was produced primarily by an influx of foreign direct investment. While EU membership may have been an element in this it is now seen by the Irish State's competitors as the means to undercut it in the race to attract foreign companies. EU membership has also contributed to the recent economic collapse as its policies helped fuel the credit–fuelled boom. Liberalisation of financial markets made it easier for Irish banks to borrow money from international sources, much of which was then lent on to property developers. German banks have lent just over €3,000 to every Greek and €2,000 to every Italian but about €42,000 for each resident of the Irish State, which means that the debt created is more than three times greater than that of Iceland to the UK and the Netherlands.[93] The introduction of the single currency in 1999, which locked Ireland into the European Central Bank's (ECB) low interest rate regime, also served to encourage domestic borrowing. It is arguable that far from the EU marking itself as an alternative model to the neoliberal US and UK the incorporation of explicitly free market liberal principles in the very constitution of the EU, especially through the Maastricht Treaty, means that 'Europe' is more fundamentalist than either.

The EU has also been instrumental in the bailout of the banks and the cuts in public spending, encouraging, cheerleading and approving both. Without the endorsement of the EU, and

---

92 Anthony Coughlan – Ireland's experience in the European Union, TCD, 03/04/00.
93 Ireland's private debt – is it time to default?, www.progressive–economy.ie.

support from the European Central Bank (ECB), NAMA could not have come into being. The cuts in public spending are also partly motivated by the requirement of euro membership through compliance with the Growth and Stability Pact which mandates budget deficits no higher than 3 per cent of GDP. Nevertheless, while the EU has undoubtedly played a role, it would be wrong to simply lay the blame for economic crisis at its door. The policies emanating from the EU and ECB support and reinforce those adopted in Ireland. It is mistaken to believe that if the State had not been in the EU, or had retained control over its currency and interest rates, that the outcome would have been radically different. We need only look at the example of Iceland, the country that Ireland has been most often compared to, to see the fallacy of this nationalistic argument.

The strategy for recovery has been described as an 'internal devaluation' because membership of the euro makes currency devaluation impossible. The primary mechanism for this is a wage reduction covering the full range of pay rates, benefits and public services. The expectation is that as wages fall so will prices, which in turn will attract foreign investment, boost Irish exports and also revive domestic markets.[94] To some degree this is an attempt to get back to the export led growth that marked the early phase of the Celtic Tiger. But how realistic is this? As we have shown earlier, export led growth was faltering by 2001 under the first shocks to globalisation. Foreign investment in the most productive sectors of the Irish economy was already starting to fall away as capital sought out even more profitable environments in Eastern Europe or China. It is questionable whether any conceivable wage reduction could restore the Irish State's attractiveness as a site for investment in comparison to these countries.

A survey on investment intentions among corporations in 15 countries, looking forward five years, found that while five or ten years ago, Ireland might have expected to feature as a preferred place to invest, for many respondents today it does

---

94 Irish recession – Is the worst over?, Socialist Party, 22/03/10.

not.[95] Without foreign investment an export led recovery is very unlikely and native owned industry, because of its relative weakness, cannot make this up. For example, of all exports from the Irish economy in 2009, only 10 per cent come from domestic producers.[96] The Irish State does not have a credible path for future development beyond dependence on foreign capital and this puts immense downward pressure and insecurity on the standard of living that can be expected if this model continues to be accepted.

It is also the case that some of the measures taken by the Government are actually compounding the problem. Cutting public spending and reducing wages have served to dampen domestic demand and consumer spending. It is estimated for example that the withdrawal of €4 billion in the December 2009 budget had a deflationary impact of 2.3 per cent on GNP.[97] Deflation has had the potential to seize up the economy, as people opt not to spend today given the expectation that prices will continue to fall and their incomes decline. This has implications for tax revenue as VAT returns fall because people are spending less. Rising unemployment means that taxes from PAYE will also go down. One third of the 'savings' generated by cutting public sector wages were lost immediately in the State's lower tax take.[98]

Importantly the 'recovery' strategy does nothing to address the country's debt crisis – private sector debt is three times GDP, while public sector debt is close to 70 per cent of GDP.[99] Deflationary policies will have the effect of increasing the burden of debt significantly because while wages and prices are declining the debt will remain the same or rise, meaning that paying it off will become more burdensome. Moreover, the escalating costs of the financial bailout will increase the overall size of debt, particularly if the Government extends

95 KPMG survey finds evidence of shift of global economic power to Emerging Asian Markets, Finfacts, 17/06/08.
96 Irish recession – Is the worst over?, Socialist Party, 22/03/10.
97 Irish recession – Is the worst over?, Socialist Party, 22/03/10.
98 Ireland's Thatcher Moment, SWP, 24/02/10.
99 Irish recession – Is the worst over?, Socialist Party, 22/03/10.

nationalisation and all the liabilities of the banks are taken on by the state. By its own stated objectives the Government and employers' recovery plan is failing, with many of the measures being pursued making the situation worse. The economy is continuing to contract,[100] and the State remains heavily indebted. In terms of protecting the Irish people the plan is a clear failure, but protecting the people has never been its objective. In terms of defending class interest and class rule it is having some success. The working class is being made to pay for the crisis as living standards are being reduced and further public resources transferred from labour to capital.

ICTU

The advances of the Government and employers' agenda have been due in no small part to the lack of an opposition. The official Dail opposition has proposed slightly different ways of bailing out the financial system but these still involve the majority paying for the reckless pursuit of profit by the few. They have therefore supported the cuts in pay and services that the governing parties have introduced. The decisive failure of opposition however has been the positive support the Government has received from the official leadership of the trade union movement.

Over 20 years of social partnership has produced a leadership that is completely integrated within the establishment consensus. Within this framework there has been room for trade union protest but the purpose of this protest has not been to build opposition but to demonstrate the ability of the trade union leaders to marshal and control workers. On regular occasions they have mustered huge protests over particular issues only to go into talks soon afterwards to 'forget' what they previously opposed and accept a new instalment of the same medicine. The classic example of this was in the Irish Ferries dispute of 2005, when over 150,000 people attended union organised rallies against the exploitation of workers at sea. Only a few days after this impressive mobilisation the trade

---

100 Economy to contract by 1.3 per cent in 2010, Irish Times, 22/03/10

union leadership made an agreement with the company that allowed it to strip its staff of almost all employment rights. The only modification was that Irish Ferries would hold off its plans for a few months.

The nature of protest within social partnership was further illustrated by trade union opposition to the 'pension levy', in reality a pure wage cut. In the previous round of partnership talks ICTU had agreed to a proposed €2 billion worth of budget cuts.[101] They baulked only at the proposal for a ten per cent pension levy because of its manifest unfairness and the negative reaction from union members. To endorse such a proposal at that point could have undermined their position. They therefore went into the now well–rehearsed routine of calling a major demonstration. Once again this showed their ability to mobilise workers, but the message to the demonstrators was not one of outright opposition to the pension levy and other attacks on workers, rather it was one of sharing the pain, a theme encapsulated in ICTU's ten point plan – "A Better Fairer Way". The opposition to the pension levy was therefore significantly dampened straight away.

The empty sabre rattling from the trade union leaders extended a little further than usual with a call for a day of action on March 30, 2009. This was to consist of strike action and protests across both the private and public sector. Yet the campaign to build for this was half hearted at best. This was reflected in the wording used on the various strike ballots. Ostensibly about the specifics of the pension levy and national pay agreement, many of the ballots made no mention of them and instead called for an endorsement of ICTU's ten–point plan – "A Better Fairer Way". The main thrust of this was acceptance of the pain but simply asking for it to be shared out between those responsible for the mess and those who were not. We therefore had the perverse situation in which workers were asked to endorse measures that they had come out to protest against in their tens of thousands just a few weeks earlier.

---

101 The last roll of the dice for Government, Ibec and unions, Irish Times, 26/03/09.

The trade union leadership never showed any intention of going ahead with the day of action and it was nothing more than a gesture to assuage the anger of the members. For the trade union leaders strike action, which carried potential for escalation, had to be avoided at all costs. The fact is that they never stopped talking to the Government despite the formal breakdown of the partnership process. The means by which the day of action was cancelled, the invitation to talks and hint of a relaxation in borrowing limits – hyped as a breakthrough by trade union leaders – was carefully choreographed between the two parties.[102]

The lack of commitment of the trade unions leaders became even more obvious after the cancellation of the day of action. Peter McLoone of Impact said that the resumption of talks had been "what the congress has been seeking all along". Irish National Teachers Organisation General Secretary John Carr said the key objective of calling the work stoppage was to get the government to re–engage with the trade unions on a social partnership basis. It had sought a mandate for industrial action not as a means of opposing the pension levy but as "leverage to secure a re–engagement with Government".[103] Teachers Union of Ireland General Secretary Peter MacMenamin welcomed the decision of the Government to "re–engage with the other social partners" and reiterated his union's support for a "fairer distribution of the effects of the economic difficulties in accordance with the ICTU's ten–point plan."[104] In all this workers were used as bargaining chips to secure trade union leaders a place around the table with the Government and employers. It was also clear that the only purpose of those new negotiations was how to impose the upcoming emergency budget in April. ICTU had already agreed to this in principal: this was the thrust of the framework document agreed between the social partners in January. Indeed, in his letter to ICTU inviting it to take part in talks, Brian Cowen said that the core elements of a new integrated national response to the economic

102 Exceeding 9.5 per cent borrowing limit 'key to new deal', Irish Times, 26/03/09.

103 Unions call off strike action and agree to enter talks, Irish Times, 25/03/09.

104 Executive Committee decides to defer strike action, TUI, 25/10/09.

and other related crises had been outlined in that document,[105] and that the new round of talks would "build on the framework . . . to see if it's possible to proceed with agreement on a range of issues."[106] Even before the talks commenced ICTU president David Begg was warning that the outcome of any agreement and the content of the emergency budget on April 7 was likely to be disappointing.[107]

Begg was certainly right about the emergency budget, which contained deep cuts in public spending, particularly in the education and health sectors and in benefits. Despite returning to talks the trade union leadership had failed to secure anything. Indeed, the lack of opposition was emboldening the Government and employers to press ahead with further attacks.

In the wake of the emergency budget and with the expectation of pay cuts in the December budget ICTU again went into the well–worn routine of protesting within social partnership. The new campaign, which was entitled 'Get Up Stand Up', and ostensibly in opposition to cuts in public services and wage reductions for public sector workers, started off with a series of demonstrations and a call for a one day strike. There was a trade union day of action on November 6 that saw tens of thousands of workers across the country attending lunchtime rallies, and a protest by members of the 'Frontline Alliance' group of trade unions in Dublin on November 11. A succession of ballots by public sector unions comprehensively endorsed the call for a one day strike on November 24.[108]

ICTU also relaunched an updated "There is A Better Fairer Way" document, which was first published in February. New additions to this included an accord which would match medium–term trends in wage cuts with those in competitor countries and proposals for the introduction of a third tax rate aimed at the wealthy which would be "up around 54 per cent". These were alongside the original proposals for tackling the

105 Government invites unions back to talks on economy, Irish Times, 24/03/09.

106 Unions call off strike action and agree to enter talks, Irish Times, 25/03/09.

107 The last roll of the dice for Government, Ibec and unions, Irish Times, 26/03/09.

108 Angry unions will bring country 'to a standstill', Irish Independent, 29/10/09.

pension crisis, reforming the banking industry and introducing legislation on workers' rights.[109] Yet it is doubtful how much trade union leaders actually supported these limited demands since their actions revealed them to be a cover for their own complicity in the polices being pursued by Government. David Begg admitted that there had not been "any move towards our position" from the Government and employers since February.[110] Despite this talks continued.

We got some indication of the substance of these talks with the publication of a letter from IMPACT general secretary Peter McLoone asking officials to identify significant and substantial costs that could be cut out of the system in order to avoid pay cuts. McLoone warned officials in his union that any deal to avoid public sector pay cuts was likely to involve reductions in the number of people employed in the public sector from 2011. He stated that the "alternative [to pay cuts] is likely to involve a significant reduction in public service numbers over the next three to four years, with the likelihood that some additional exceptional measures will also be needed in 2010 to deal with the budgetary crisis next year."[111] The message to Government and workers was clear: the trade union leaders had accepted the cuts and were presenting their members with a 'choice' between redundancies and pay cuts.

In a rerun of February's day of action a planned national strike was called off as trade union leaders reached a tentative agreement with the Government on reducing the public pay bill. Again this should have come as no surprise. The trade union leadership had implicitly accepted a service cutting agenda from the outset, the only question was how it was to be implemented and what face saving measures could be employed to sell it to the membership. On the issue of reducing the pay bill, the unions pushed for unpaid leave as an alternative to pay cuts but any claimed distinction between unpaid leave and pay cuts was really false. The rates of pay may have remained the same, but the reduction in working days would still result in a wage cut.

---

109 Ictu calls for spending cuts to be deferred, Irish Times, 03/11/09.
110 Ictu calls for spending cuts to be deferred, Irish Times, 03/11/09.
111 Government and unions resume public sector talks, Irish Times, 03/11/09.

This concentration on pay rates had long been a feature of the trade union approach to negotiations, as working conditions and jobs were sacrificed to preserve headline pay. As long as the pay rate was preserved trade union leaders could claim a success. Of course this success was totally illusory as it inevitably resulted in job losses and deteriorating conditions and now even to reductions in pay.

The draft agreement reached on the cuts in the public sector pay bill bore all the hallmarks of this approach. It proposed the introduction of a twelve and a half days unpaid leave scheme which would produce savings in the following year.[112] This was the equivalent of a seven per cent pay cut for the average worker, coming on top of an effective 7.5 per cent cut in take–home pay from the pension levy in February, and the suspension of the 2.5 per cent increase due under the national pay accord in October.[113] The second element of the draft agreement promoted an overall transformation of the public sector commencing in 2011. This "reform strand", which was to be the subject of forthcoming talks, was based on a recently published Government document that envisaged a much smaller public sector in the years ahead. The underlying principal of this document was that public services, which were already underfunded, would have to do more with fewer resources. It indicated that the number of staff on the state payroll would fall substantially and that the existing moratorium on recruitment in the public service would remain until 2014. It also proposed a voluntary redundancy scheme and further casualisation of employment, with the abolition of shift and overtime premiums and compulsory redeployments.[114]

What was particularly noteworthy about the suspension of the strike and the capitulation of the trade union leadership was that it followed on from a relatively successful, in terms of participation at least, one day public sector strike. On November 24 much of the public sector was shut down as nurses, teachers, firefighters and other employees protested

---

112 Union chief concedes that €1.3 billion payroll cut is needed , Irish Independent, 25/11/09.

113 Irish public sector workers strike, Financial Times, 24/11/09.

114 Government and unions consider the alternatives, Irish Times, 25/11/09.

against Government plans to cut pay. There were a number of lively demonstrations, such as the march by primary school teachers to the Department of Education headquarters in Dublin.[115] The spirit displayed by pickets and demonstrators was not however reflected in the trade union leadership. Its negotiating team was desperate to avoid strike action. For them strike action was not a means of challenging the Government but of showing the value of continuing with a social partnership that severely controlled it. They were desperate for an agreement and over the course of the period, between the first strike day and the scheduled second day of strikes, became more explicit in their willingness to accept the Government's proposals. Speaking as 250,000 workers effectively closed down the entire public service for 24 hours, ICTU's lead negotiator Peter McLoone said it would be necessary to agree temporary measures to cut the payroll next year. He also said a Government document on transforming public services could form the basis of negotiations, and that it would be "possible to agree an alternative that will achieve the savings the Government requires."[116] This was followed by a speech by Jack O'Connor of the Services Industrial Professional and Technical Union (SIPTU) in which he called for consideration to be given to adjusting pay levels, arguing that the "boom has disproportionately increased pay and pay costs here as against competitor countries."[117] Trade union leaders were now openly calling for pay cuts.

Even this capitulation wasn't enough as the Government proceeded with its own proposals to cut pay. The mechanism that the trade union leadership hoped would achieve this would have reduced overall pay while leaving pay rates intact. A secondary element was agreement on the complete overhaul of pay and working conditions within the public sector from 2011. The net effect would have been an immediate five percent pay cut for the public sector with a wholesale assault on conditions to follow, and all for a face saving gesture of maintaining pay rates for a short period.

---

115 Unions announce second day of strikes for next week, Irish Times , 24/11/09.

116 Union chief concedes that €1.3 billion payroll cut is needed , Irish Independent, 25/11/09.

117 Union leader says pay rose too much in boom, Irish Times, 27/10/09.

The trade union leaders did their best to talk this proposal up as a major breakthrough but hopes for an agreement were dashed when it was rejected by the Government. There was speculation that the Government never seriously considered the paid leave proposal or was using the talks to draw out what the unions would agree to in a future overhaul of the public sector, one that they could commence negotiations from later. In the end the convoluted proposals of the trade unions were rejected in favour of a straight pay cut. Trade union leaders were indignant that agreement had not been reached. The unions' chief negotiator, Peter McLoone, said he was "deeply disappointed and astonished" that the opportunity for transforming the public services had been allowed to slip away. He claimed that the aborted deal would have delivered "a massive transformation in the delivery of public services far beyond anything previously contemplated – let alone achieved – in this state."[118]

Despite their public indignation and claims that the proposed deal on public sector reform was "dead and buried" it remained very much on the agenda. As one government official said: "They've put out the list of things they said they would do. Why don't they go ahead and do them [in the interests of a better public service]? Do it anyway."[119] Even in the wake of the Government announcement that it was to press ahead with the pay cuts, trade union leaders continued to cling to social partnership. Jack O'Connor said there was "some possibility" of retrieving ground "if something progressive "was done to make the budget fair.[120] This was quickly dashed with the publication of a budget containing €4 billion worth of cuts made up mostly of pay and welfare reductions.

The start of the year in 2010 saw the launch of another campaign of action against the imposition of public sector pay cuts. The strategy behind this campaign was set out in a document published by ICTU's Public Services Committee. It centred on public sector workers engaging in a form of low

118 Government sacrificing reform on altar of pay cuts, Irish Times, 08/11/09.

119 Pay cut law was in place before talks collapsed, Sunday Business Post, 05/12/09.

120 Unions warn of public service 'campaign' against pay cuts, Irish Times, 08/12/09.

intensity industrial struggle with the Governement. The campaign included non–co–operation with management reforms such as redeployment and action in all sectors, including schools, colleges, hospitals, and public offices. Alongside an immediate work to rule the strategy document set out a number of other tactics, including selective strike action to be used intermittently; the possiblity of a one–day national strike at a "strategic point" in the campaign; refusal to engage with the Government's plan to "transform" the public sector; demonstrations and protests; industrial action where there was a threat of compulsory redundancies or disciplinary action due to non–co–operation; political lobbying and possible legal action over pay cuts or changes to pensions.[121]

While the strategy for the campaign outlined a range of options, up to and including a national strike, it was clear that union leaders wanted to keep action at the most minimal level possible. This reflected a need for them to be seen to be doing something in response to the attacks on their members while at the same dampening down anything that could escalate and risk a real clash with the Government. So at the same time as ICTU was launching its campaign, officials were offering assurances to employers on how limited it would be. One unnamed official was quoted as saying that among the leadership there was "no sense that there will be any escalation, apart from work–to–rules." They were taking the view that it was "a long term campaign" and there would be "no knee–jerk actions." [122] What really exposed the lack of seriousness of the campaign was the policy of non–cooperation with the Government's reform programme. It was only in the previous November that unions had offered a blank cheque on public sector reform, essentially a complete overhaul of pay and working conditions, as part of an aborted deal on unpaid leave.

The approach of the trade union leaders was summed up in Jack O'Connor's claim that "In order to make peace we have to prepare for war."[123] On the face of it such statements sounded

---

121 Unions wage 'cold war' in first phase of pay–cut battle, Irish Independent, 08/01/10.

122 Unions reluctant to unleash full–scale strikes, Sunday Business Post, 24/01/10.

123 Ictu outlines programme of industrial action, Irish Times, 08/01/10.

quite militant, but in reality they were the same old empty sabre rattling that trade union leaders had engaged in for years. There had been no shift within the trade unions after the collapse of formal partnership arrangements the previous December. There was no sense that the trade union leadership were preparing for class war. The most they were contemplating were a few minor skirmishes ahead of a hoped for restoration of some form of partnership. Indeed, the latest campaign was framed in terms of securing a new agreement. That is why alongside the bellicose rhetoric we had Jack O'Connor holding out the prospect of a deal allowing for the transformation of public services. He stated explicitly that the aim of the industrial action campaign was to persuade the Government to negotiate an alternative to the 'Towards 2016' partnership agreement which had been reneged upon.[124]

So once again while partnership was pronounced dead, and a campaign organised, there were moves towards a deal which betrayed its objectives. The Government signalled that it would consider reversing some element of the public service pay cuts in the following year's budget, or at least not make further cuts, provided the savings could be secured in major reform and efficiencies. The Chief Executive of the Labour Relations Commission (LRC) Kieran Mulvey met with government officials to assess if there was a basis for employers and unions to restart negotiations. The conciliatory noises from Government were leapt upon by the trade unions. IMPACT General Secretary Peter McLoone said that "if the government was opening the door for negotiations on the basis of reforms it would be a positive step."[125]

Not surprisingly, the trade union leadership agreed in early March to return to negotiations.[126] The campaign of a work to rule that had been engaged in was never going to elicit any changes in Government policy, and indeed was not seriously meant to. Once again it was an exercise in marching the membership, not so much up and down the hill as round and

124 O'Connor says 'determined' action needed to attain deal, Irish Times, 18/01/10.
125 Government signals pay flexibility in bid to woo unions, Sunday Business Post, 31/01/10.
126 Unions agree not to escalate action as talks renewed, Irish Times, 13/03/10.

round it. It left small groups of workers isolated and exposed to the now well established and vicious campaign against public sector workers. In just 18 months the robber bankers had moved well down the list of media hate figures to be replaced by public sector workers, pilloried for having cushy jobs with total job security, fat pensions and vertigo inducing levels of pay. The crisis of public finances was now their fault. The €82,875,000,000 to be paid to the banks? Well, even to ask the question was treated by the Government as a sign of economic illiteracy and total ignorance. In these circumstances, to challenge the Government required an alternative, an alternative ICTU didn't have, they didn't have a better or fairer way.

When it went into another round of talks the agenda had only one item – continuing cuts in public spending. Even before they commenced Jack O'Connor conceded that this was the case.[127] Indeed, it was the trade union leaders themselves, by setting out in detail what they were willing to concede in the aborted deal on unpaid leave, who provided the bulk of this agenda. The subsequent deal included a commitment by Government that there would be no more public sector pay cuts until 2014 but only if Government finances allowed, so there was in reality no firm commitment. This likewise applied to Government promises to review pay and reverse previous pay cuts if savings produced by the agreement produced the required reductions in costs. In return, the union leaders agreed to significant restructuring and reorganisation of services involving cuts in jobs and services and terms and conditions across the public sector. It agreed to a no strike deal and no future cost increasing claims for the duration of the agreement. So on top of all the previous cuts in living standards the union leaders agreed to yet more, in fact a blank cheque to gut much of the public sector, with a promise they would do nothing to try to reverse previous cuts or obstruct the new ones. With the bill still largely to hit public finances only the terminally stupid could think that any pay cuts would soon be

---

127 Ictu issues warning on pay talks, Irish Times, 14/03/10.

reversed as part of the deal. The only question that remained was whether the union leadership could sell it to their membership.

The actions and words of trade union leaders have displayed a grim determination to stick with partnership which has contrasted sharply with the complete absence of determination when defending their members. They know nothing else but partnership and find it impossible to envision the trade union movement playing an independent role. On the other hand the Government has shown extraordinary energy in attempting to save bankers and developers, no matter what the risk and no matter what the cost. In the next chapter we look more closely at this attempt and in the following at the rather different approach taken by ICTU in representing the interests of working people. In the final chapter we present what would actually amount to an alternative.

Chapter 2

The NAMA Cure:
Bleeding the Patient

"This bank bailout is a simple transfer from taxpayers to bondholders, and it will saddle generations to come. The only thing that might give you solace is that, as chief economist of the World Bank, we see this type of thing happening in banana republics all over the world. Whenever a banking crisis happens, the financial sector uses the turmoil as a mechanism to transfer wealth from the general population to themselves"[128]

This assessment was made by Nobel Prize winner and former chief economist of the World Bank Professor Joe Stiglitz on an engagement in Dublin, providing a succinct summary of the Government's plans for the rescue of the Irish banking sector. He correctly identified it as a bailout in which wealth is transferred from one section of the population to another, or more accurately from one class to another –– from the working class to the capitalist class. The "mechanism" through which it is carried out is the National Asset Management Agency (NAMA).

The immediate reason for the establishment of NAMA was the failure of all the other methods deployed by the Government to halt the collapse of Irish banks and building societies. They had

---

128 Joe Stiglitz quoted in 'Nama is highway robbery', David McWilliams Blog, 12/10/09.

been hit by the world–wide financial crisis of 2008, but even had this not occurred, the collapse of the domestic property market in which so much of their investment had been concentrated would have dragged them down anyway. The growth of the property sector over the previous decade had largely been credit led – it was not a reflection of growing commercial or residential demand but of speculative investment, the motor for which was the expansion of bank lending. The Irish State went from getting four to six per cent of its national income from house building in the 1990s – the usual level for a developed economy – to 15 per cent at the peak of the bubble in 2006–07, with another six per cent coming from other construction.[129] Irish bank lending, mostly developer loans and mortgages, grew almost seven–fold to €400 billion in the ten years after joining the euro at the beginning of 1999.[130] In 2008, it reached 200 per cent of national income.[131] This expansion of lending had the effect of dramatically ramping up property prices – between 2000 and 2006 house prices doubled relative to income and rents.[132] Such speculative growth however has a limit as a point is reached when borrowings become unsustainable from existing income. When this happens the upward spiral of increasing borrowing and rising prices starts to work in reverse. The notion put about to assuage doubters that everyone was heading for a 'soft landing' was always false.

The financial crisis in Ireland had its own particular dynamic, and was not merely a consequence of the meltdown elsewhere, even if its essential characteristics, resulting from an irrational economic system, were the same. Indeed, Ireland's tipping point predated the global financial crash. The average size of mortgages approved had peaked in the third quarter of 2006. By the middle of 2007 the construction industry was in decline as unsold units began to accumulate. This slowdown in the property market impacted on the State's heavily exposed banks. Their assets were dramatically degraded as property values fell

129 Morgan Kelly – The Irish Credit Bubble – WP09/32, UCD Centre for Economic Research, December 2009.
130 Rogue banks cost us all a fortune. So who was protecting them?, Herald, 22/12/09.
131 Kelly, December 2009.
132 Best to ignore the cheerleaders for the property sector, Southern Star, 31/12/09.

and the repayment of loans was put in doubt. This was reflected in the collapse in their share price as investors and money markets withdrew support; a process which came to a head in late September 2008 with a run in wholesale markets on the joint–second largest Irish bank, Anglo Irish.[133] A large section of the financial sector was on the brink of bankruptcy. In response to this the Government made a series of interventions including the beggar thy neighbour policy of the 100% deposit guarantee; a round of recapitalisation which injected over €10 billion into the system;[134] and the nationalisation of Anglo Irish Bank. Each intervention confirmed the failure of the previous, although always denied.

Draft legislation

It was on the back of the failure to alleviate the crisis that the idea of the establishment a state run 'bad bank' which would take on the toxic assets held by the commercial banks, started to gain currency. In February 2009, the Government appointed economist Peter Bacon to assess the possibility of creating such a bank or risk insurance scheme[135]and acting on his report, began preparations to establish a bad loans agency to cleanse the banks of their toxic assets.[136] This took a more concrete form in August 2009 with the publication of the draft legislation to establish NAMA, which envisioned the Government purchasing loans with a face value of up to €90 billion from the banks.[137]

The new agency would take control of the loans and the associated charges which had been pledged as security against the loans, holding them until the market improved whereupon they could be sold and its investment recouped. The transfer of assets to NAMA would be achieved through the issuing of Government bonds that would be used to buy the property loans at a discounted rate from the banks, which could then

---

133 Kelly, December 2009.

134 Government looking for a 'blank cheque' from taxpayers, Irish Times, 31/07/09.

135 State hires Bacon for 'bad bank' role, Irish Times, 20/02/09.

136 Annus horribilis for Irish banks, Irish Times, 31/12/09.

137 Taxpayers can't lumped with shareholders win, Herald, 31/07/09.

cash the bonds with the European Central Bank. The claim made for this process was that it would restore liquidity to the banks, enabling them to start lending again and thereby hastening the pace of economic recovery. According to Finance Minister Brian Lenihan, this had to be done to put the banks in "a position to be the motor of credit in our economy".[138]

He made it clear that it was the public who had "to pick up the bill here to ensure a viable bank system" although at this stage it was not clear what that bill would amount to.[139] The draft legislation omitted one critical element – how much would be paid to the banks for the loans. The Government indicated that it would not pay the value at which the loans were made (€90 billion), but neither would it pay the current market value, which after the collapse of the property market, stood at perhaps around €40 billion, although no one could really know, since who could know what any one asset might be worth if they were all sold onto the market. The higher the valuation of the loans the greater the benefit to the banks and the greater the risk taken on by the public as taxpayer.

Lenihan introduced the concept "long–term economic value"[140] to justify not paying the current market rate, and prepare the ground for a price much higher in the range. Of course "long–term economic value" could almost be whatever the Government wanted it to be – there was no way to accurately calculate what the value of the loans would be in five or ten years, even with so called expert scrutiny of the loans. This was recognised by IMF officials who praised the concept as "masterful" for being "sufficiently specific" and "sufficiently vague" to allow "appropriate flexibility".[141]

Despite bullish statements coming from ministers, officials had already conceded that there would be a loss on NAMA. A memorandum from the Department of Finance admitted that the long–term value of the assets to be transferred from the

---

138 It could take 30 years to sort out this mess, Irish Independent, 31/07/09.

139 'We must pick up bill to get viable banking', Herald, 31/07/09.

140 Lenihan fails to reveal 'haircut' applying to bad loans, Irish Times, 31/07/09.

141 Nama definition of 'long–term value' masterful, says IMF, Irish Times, 19/12/09.

banks would be "significantly less than the outstanding loan."[142] The question was not whether there would be a loss but how great that loss would be. Bank analysts and economists estimated that the 'haircut' that the banks would have to take – the discount that would be applied to their loan portfolios – would be less than 25 per cent of the loans' value. It was expected that the Government would pay about €60 billion or €70 billion for them – handing a gift of €20 to €30 billion of public money to the bankers.[143] The corollary of this was that the public could incur a loss of up to the same amount. Given that the whole NAMA process was about bailing out the banks it couldn't really be any other way.

The Carroll case

While ministers talked up the value of the assets that would be taken into NAMA and commentators speculated on the costs of the scheme, a series of court cases involving one of the country's biggest property developers started to quantify the liabilities that would be involved. The legal action came about as a result of Liam Carroll's Zoe group being unable to repay a loan to the Dutch owned AAC bank. When demand letters were issued Carroll made an application to the High Court for protection. The court refused to extend protection and instead appointed an examiner to six companies in the Zoe group. This process culminated in the Supreme Court with Carroll's failed attempt to have the High Court judgement overturned. ACC was granted a series of orders it was seeking to recover the €136m owed to it by the Zoe group.[144]

While the ACC bank was a relatively small player its decision to pursue Carroll put a spotlight on the whole rotten structure of the Irish property market. It also made public some facts about the property sector that the Government, banks and developers had preferred remained secret. This came at a particularly sensitive time with the Government bringing forward its plans

---

142 'Nationalisation' bobs on the horizon, Irish Independent, 02/08/09.

143 Lenihan must save banking not bankers, Sunday Independent, 02/0809.

144 Carroll creditor banks hold emergency meeting, Irish Times, 13/08/09.

for the bad bank that would take the high-risk loans from banks and transfer the liability to the State. The claim made for the plan was that the value of the assets on which the loans were secured, while currently low, would recover over time and thereby minimise any losses. The examination of Carroll's affairs by the courts revealed such positive projections to be totally baseless.

Liam Carroll owed over €2.5 billion to the banks, Irish owned banks accounting for the bulk of this. His Zoe group owed €1.2 billion to eight banks including ACC.[145] Given the overall size of Carroll's property empire, and the size of the part of it that was under scrutiny, it could be assumed that what was revealed about the state of his companies was a fairly accurate picture of the wider property sector. Indeed, as most of their property was located in and around Dublin, Carroll's companies were probably in a better state than those of most developers.[146]

The argument that Carroll made to forestall his creditors, which was essentially the same as the one made by the Government for NAMA, was that the value of his assets would rise in the near future and allow him to pay back his loans. His business plan however lacked any credibility. How the fortunes of the Zoe companies could be transformed from insolvency and a deficit of more than €1 billion into a €290 million surplus in three years, and in a depressed property market, was never clearly established to the court's satisfaction.[147] The judge dismissed the plan, describing it as "fanciful", "lacking in reality" and containing "something artificial".[148]

The Carroll case also highlighted the deliberately complex structure and financing of Irish property companies. Across the Zoe group there was a high level of cross ownership and intermingling of debt. Vantive Holdings and Jersey-registered Morston Investments sat at the apex of about 50 subsidiaries in

---

145 Contagion effect of liquidation of Zoe companies is massive, Irish Times, 13/08/09.
146 Carroll saga reveals unholy pact between bankers and developers, Irish Times, 13/08/09.
147 Nama after the Carroll case, Irish Times, 13/08/09.
148 Only one thing to do if Liam Carroll loses tomorrow - panic, Irish Independent, 03/08/09.

the group.[149] Documents lodged with the Companies' Registration Office (CRO) showed that, along with another Jersey–based vehicle, Stradbally Investments, Vantive was a shareholder in Peytor Developments and Villeer Developments. In turn, Peytor was the sole shareholder in Parlez International and Carragh Enterprises. Along with this, Morston and Stradbally were shareholders in Vantive. The CRO records showed that Vantive, Peytor, Villeer, Carragh and Parlez, all owed debts to a series of banks, which were secured against properties in the Castleforbes–Upper Sherriff Street area on the north side of Dublin's docklands.[150]

While Vantive and Morston had their own problems with respective deficits of €396 million and €361 million on liquidation, they also had colossal exposure on inter–company debts and guarantees across Carroll's groups. Companies throughout Carroll's group owed €569.9 million to Vantive which had in turn guaranteed debts of €224.4 million. There was also a heavy intermingling of debts across Carroll's Zoe group and his other two groups, Dunloe and Orthanc, and the three altogether owed an estimated €2.8 billion.[151] This created the potential for a domino effect of defaults, liquidation and selloffs across his entire business. Such a scenario would also have had a major impact on the wider property and banking sector as companies were liquidated and the fire sale of their assets pushed property values down even further.

The Carroll case and its outworking gave the first clear picture of the likely financial state of Irish property companies whose loans NAMA was supposed to purchase. During the High Court case Carroll's accountants admitted that his Zoe group could only pay back about one–quarter of the money it owed to the Irish banks.[152] If NAMA purchased loans for an average discount of one quarter, paying 75 per cent of the original value of the loans, the State would be paying three times the amount that they could be sold to anyone else.

149 Contagion effect of liquidation of Zoe companies is massive, Irish Times, 13/08/09.
150 Finding out firms' interests a difficult exercise, Irish Times, 13/12/09.
151 Carroll creditor banks hold emergency meeting, Irish Times, 13/08/09.
152 Fallout from Zoe collapse poses problems for Nama, Irish Times, 20/07/09.

The case also exposed the corrupt relationship between the banks, developers and politicians. Despite the reality that Carroll's business simply could not be saved, all the Irish banks involved actively supported this survival plan,[153] allowing Carroll to continue rolling up interest and also taking the highly unusual step of providing the funds to pay off unsecured trade creditors. The banks were determined to maintain the illusion that Carroll could pay back the money he owed, with the prospect of the creation of a bad bank providing a big incentive for this. With the Finance Minister signalling his determination to take a positive view of all loan purchases (emphasising their "long–term economic value") participating banks were encouraged to maintain that loans such as Carroll's were good just long enough for them to be sold to NAMA for far more than they would ever repay. This manoeuvring by the banks only came into the public realm because the Dutch–owned ACC was left out of NAMA and so didn't have any incentive to go along with the pretence over the value of Carroll's loans.

These court proceedings served to lay bare the true state of the property market and the scandalous nature of the efforts to bail out the banks and the developers. The Government and bank bosses were nevertheless completely dismissive of the public concerns that had been raised. Their attitude was summed up by Frank O'Dwyer, chair of the Irish Association of Investment Managers and key government adviser, who asserted that an "excessive haircut, with any taint of political motivation [and] any sense of 'let's stick it to these guys' would erode confidence".[154] Of course it wasn't the confidence of the Irish people he was referring to. For him the "the key audience" was "international financial markets."[155]

Valuation of loans

Confirmation that NAMA would be a mechanism to bail out the

153 Carroll failure a service to State, Irish Independent, 17/08/09.
154 Carroll creditor banks hold emergency meeting, Irish Times, 13/08/09.
155 Nama may pay €40 billion over the odds, Sunday Independent, 16/08/09.

banks came on September 16, 2009, when the Finance Minister announced how much it expected to pay to transfer the loans to the new agency. The figures came during the opening of the Dail debate on the legislation that would pave the way for its creation. He announced that NAMA would take €77 billion worth of loans off the banks, with the state paying around €54 billion – a discount of around 30 per cent. His department estimated that the current value of these properties, if they were to be put on the market, would be in the region of €47 billion – a write–down of 47 per cent.[156] It estimated that, in the long term, in other words, in about seven to ten years, it was reasonable to expect that they might be worth €54 billion, the so–called long–term economic value of the assets. The minister even claimed that NAMA could break even if the properties rose in value by around 10 per cent over the coming decade.[157] On these figures there was only a €7 billion gap between the current value of the assets and the amount that was to be paid for them. Given the speculation that had appeared in the media prior to the debate the figures didn't seem so bad. When the figures were examined in closer detail however, it was clear that the costs and potential risks of NAMA had not been reduced. The Government had simply concealed them by making a number of unfounded assumptions and engaging in a financial sleight of hand.

Firstly, there was the estimate of the current market value of the assets related to the loans that were to be taken over. The Finance Minister estimated that these assets had fallen in value by 47 per cent, leaving them with a market value of €47 billion; but how accurate was this? The NAMA loans were divided into three categories – landbank, development and associated loans. Landbank accounted for 36 per cent of the total; development loans accounted for 28 per cent and associated loans (mainly commercial properties, such as office blocks, retail buildings, hotels etc) accounted for 36 per cent. Given that the total value of these projects was €88.3 billion (the value of the property on which the loans were secured), then the original value of the

---

156 Nama smoke begins to clear, Sunday Business Post, 20/09/09.

157 Success or failure of scheme hinges on future of the property market, Irish Times, 17/09/09.

land bank was around €31.7 billion, development projects approximately €24.7 billion and the others around €31.7 billion.[158]

But what were they worth now? According to Savills summer 2009 property review, land bank values had fallen by between 30 per cent and 90 per cent from their peak. Danske Bank reported that some sites in Ireland had fallen in value by 80 per cent. Home-builder McInerney Holdings had written down the value of its land bank by 52 per cent, while Davy Stockbrokers had written down the value of its client's investment in the Irish Glass Bottle site by 60 per cent, and the former Cahill Printers site in East Wall in Dublin by 90 per cent. Based on these deals land bank prices had fallen in value by 60 per cent since their peak – and that would be a conservative estimate. This meant that the original land in the NAMA portfolio may have fallen from €31.7 billion to €12.6 billion.

The value of development projects had fallen by at a much greater amount. During the Carroll case, the legal team acting for his Zoe group of companies admitted that a sale of the group's assets would raise only €300 million of the €1.2 billion it owed. This represented a 75 per cent fall in the value of Carroll's assets. Given the size of this property empire this could be fairly representative of the sector as a whole. The third element of the NAMA loans was associated loans made to big developers, secured on commercial properties such as shopping centres, office blocks and hotels. These are buildings that are finished and are generating a revenue stream, and are probably the best loans on the best properties going to NAMA. But even they had seen their value fall, with commercial property down by around 50 per cent from its peak.[159] Taken together, and based on a conservative estimate of a 60 per cent fall from peak for the land and development projects and a 47 per cent fall for the others, this left the current market value of the NAMA assets at €39 billion, not the €47 billion claimed by the Government.

---

158 Do the Nama property sums add up?, Sunday Business Post, 20/09/09.
159 Ibid.

On these estimates the gap between what might be paid for the assets and what they were worth increased to €15 billion.[160]

The second concealed cost of NAMA lay in the bonds that the Government said it would be using to purchase the loans from the banks. The Government would exchange bonds for the loans and the banks could then use these bonds to borrow from the European Central Bank. However, this could not be free money – the Irish Government had to pay interest on these bonds. NAMA bonds would have an interest rate set at a half percent above the ECB's main refinancing rate. While the ECB rate was one percent it was expected to rise over the next few years. The amount of interest paid on NAMA bonds could increase significantly as those rates rose.[161]

The third concealed cost of NAMA would be the inevitable further round of recapitalisation of the banks.[162] It may have thrown people a little than the Government left some of the toxic loans on their books rather than taking the full €90 billion worth into NAMA but this was really a sleight of hand designed to bring down the headline total. In the case of the nationalised Anglo–Irish the public had already taken on its full loan book. NAMA moving into operation would be the trigger for the banks to declare losses on the bad loans left on the books and appeal for new capital. AIB had already said that it needed €2 billion in new capital and it was estimated that Anglo–Irish needed an additional €4 billion to continue to operate.[163] This might rise to €6 billion or more due to further write–downs on loans not transferred to NAMA.[164] If these costs were added together – the inflated estimate of asset values; the interest paid on bonds; and the further recapitalisation – they were not far off earlier estimates of what NAMA would cost, with potential liabilities getting up towards €30 billion.

---

160 Ibid.

161 NAMA bond yield formula finally revealed, Irish Economy Blog, 17/09/09.

162 Ryan predicts increased State ownership of banks, Irish Times, 19/09/09.

163 Nama smoke begins to clear, Sunday Business Post, 20/09/09.

164 State faces new Anglo cash call, Sunday Business Post, 20/09/09.

The one gesture toward equity in the NAMA legislation, and for which the Green Party claimed credit,[165] was its provisions on risk sharing. This involved holding back €3 billion of the €54 billion paid for the toxic loans if NAMA didn't break even.[166] This represented about five per cent of the total issue and less than 40 per cent of the €7 billion difference resulting from the estimation of long–term value.[167] The grossly one–sided nature of this, €51 billion for the banks opposed to €3 billion for the public, only served to highlight its inequity. This so–called risk–sharing was meaningless anyway. It assumed that the Government would at some point do the opposite of what it had been doing, and which was the whole purpose of NAMA: get the banks to pay for the losses of the State.

Despite the deliberately misleading way the costs of NAMA were calculated and presented there was no hiding the fact that it was a bailout for the banks. When opening the debate on the legislation Brian Cowen had the gall to deny that this was the case.[168] The reaction of the stock market told a different story, with the prices of Irish bank shares shooting upwards. Reports of Irish property developers organising a "NAMA celebration" in Spain was another indication of who the beneficiaries were. [169] This was also reflected in the assessment of 'The Economist' magazine which commented that in its valuation of the bank loans the Government had "erred on the side of favouring shareholders."[170] The announcement of September 16 was a clear demonstration of the approach of the Irish political class to the economic crisis. The capitalist class who bore responsibility for bringing it about were to be bailed out while workers would be made to bear the cost. The whole exercise made those who deny that class rule or class struggle exist look either wilfully naive or simply cynical.

---

165 Changes needed to ensure fair valuations, says Ryan, Irish Independent, 17/09/09.

166 Taxpayers at risk for billions after risk–sharing is scaled back, Irish Times, 17/09/09.

167 Banks' exposure of 5% on €54billion bond issue too low, say critics, Irish Times, 17/09/09.

168 Cowen denies Nama a 'bailout', Irish Times, 17/09/09.

169 Nama is a huge bail–out, whatever Cowen claims, Sunday Independent, 20/09/09.

170 The Morning After, Economist, 17/09/09.

NAMA business plan

Further details on how NAMA would operate came in October 2009 when the Finance Minister unveiled its business plan. This was accompanied by increasingly bullish projections on how the agency would perform. Previously the Government had claimed that a recovery in asset prices of 10 per cent over the ten-year lifetime of NAMA would enable the agency to avoid a loss. Now the claim was that by 2020, when NAMA was expected to be wound up, the agency would have returned a profit of €5.48 billion, which after projected inflation amounted to €4.8 billion.[171]

To arrive at this figure a number of assumptions were made. Firstly, that the valuation of the loans was accurate; secondly, that there would be a recovery in the value of the property that underpinned most of these loans; and thirdly, that the default rate on loans would only be 20 per cent. All these assumptions were without foundation. The valuation put on the loans by the Government bore no relation to their current value or their likely future value. The 30 per cent discount on the loans announced in September was all about leaving the banks with enough capital to prevent them falling into insolvency. Current market transactions, along with the information that came out of the Carroll case, demonstrated that the value of these assets had fallen by up to sixty per cent, more than twice the Government's estimate. The admission that officials had not even got round to examining the individual loan files, and were relying on data supplied by the banks,[172] emphasised both the arbitrary nature of the Government's figures and that it was being driven foremost by the banks themselves.

The assumption on the default rate was also arbitrary. Officials expected that of the €77 billion loans transferred to NAMA, €62 billion would be repaid and €15 billion would not. That's 20 per cent of the loans defaulting, with the other 80 per cent

---

171 Draft NAMA business plan the details, RTÉ Business, 15/10/09.
172 Nama team still haven't seen €77 billion loan files, Irish Examiner, 15/10/09.

eventually paying off in full.[173] These figures were not based on current conditions in Ireland but on a comparison with the performance of Barclays Bank during the property slump in the UK in the early 1990s. It assumed that because the default rate on Barclays' loan book at that time was less than 10 per cent the default rate on NAMA's assets would be 20 per cent. Again this bore no relation to current conditions, which were much more severe than those in the UK twenty years ago. It is likely that far more than 20 per cent of these loans will fail to be paid back in full.[174] The bogus nature of NAMA's business plan was summed up well by the economist Morgan Kelly: "When you have every assumption like that, you no longer have a forecast, you have a fantasy."[175]

Although most of the attention had focused on the banks, the degree to which NAMA was also a bailout for the property developers became clearer with publication of the business plan. Despite talk of rigorously pursuing debtors, most of whom are developers, the timetable for debt recovery was very lax; only €1 billion of €77 billion owed would be recovered in both 2010 and 2011, with €2.5 billion recovered in 2012. This jumps to €7.5 billion in 2013. There were therefore no plans to recover the bulk of the money any time soon.[176]

So NAMA aided developers by protecting them from their creditors and artificially maintaining the value of their properties. The business plan also held out the prospect of further loans being extended to developers to fund the completion of some unfinished developments. So not only was the value of their properties being artificially preserved, it was being enhanced. In the draft NAMA Bill the amount that could be borrowed for such purposes was set at €5 billion, but in the final legislation this limit was removed.[177] The Government, or rather working people, were to finance yet further speculation.

173 Nama profit of expected by 2020, Irish Times, 15/10/09.
174 NAMA Business Plan Default Rate Assumptions, Irish Economy Blog, 15/10/09.
175 Nama 'won't revitalise banks', Irish Times, 17/10/09.
176 Hard to deny now that NAMA is a developer rescue plan, Irish Economy Blog, 15/10/09.
177 Joint ventures likely to develop sites, Irish Times, 15/10/09.

A secondary beneficiary of NAMA, after the bankers and property developers, will be that layer of property related professionals who gorged themselves during the period of the boom and were so closely implicated in its collapse. The allocation of €2.64 billion for "professional fees" associated with the operation of NAMA will create a money trough for an array of solicitors, barristers, bankers, accountants, estate agents, auctioneers and liquidators. They will be able to draw down on €240 million a year over the 10-year life of the agency.[178] These fees will be paid at every step of the convoluted process of placing a value on the loans transferred from the banks. Firstly, the banks will have to get valuations of their loans; these will then be checked by valuers employed by NAMA; legal advisors will then have to check the documentation related to the loans; other advisers – called loan valuation firms – will then put an overall value on the loans. Finally, the whole process will be audited by yet more advisors. NAMA, both directly and indirectly, will be the single biggest employer of professionals over the next ten years, with a significant layer of the middle class dependent upon it for their livelihoods.[179] Of course these professional services are a scam. The valuation of loans will not be based on objective standards but the arbitrary measurement of what will be required to preserve the banks and property developers. To value one loan requires a notion of the value of all property, in effect of all the loans, and to do this is a political decision dressed up with figures and calculations. The purpose of employing such an array of professionals is to give a veneer of independence and legality to the whole process, and also to look after a social layer that is an important source of support for the State.

One of the features of NAMA has been its anything but transparent character, arising both out of the claims made for it and the changes that have been made in its proposed operation and structure. A good example of this came during the Dail debate when it was revealed that the Government would be creating a Special Purpose Vehicle (SPV) to manage NAMA.

---

178 Nama is dead - we're on a special purpose vehicle, Sunday Business Post, 01/11/09.
179 Nama must not become a bonanza for advisers, Irish Times, 26/10/09.

This altered the nature of the agency that was to be created by the legislation under debate. It is this SPV that would have the authority and take the decisions on the bad loans and their accompanying assets to be transferred from the banks. The critical difference is that while NAMA was envisioned as entirely a state agency, this SPV would have a majority private ownership. Private investors, who would be drawn from the banking sector, would have 51 per cent of the equity of the SPV while the state would have 49 per cent. The minority State Directors would be able to veto decisions by the SPV board that they didn't like but otherwise would cede control. While the chair of NAMA will head up the SPV he will be subordinate to the will of the majority on the SPV board.

All this flew in the face of guarantees about how NAMA would be accountable to a committee of the Dail and so forth. The SPV will be a privately–controlled company accountable to no one other than its shareholders, i.e. the Government and the banks.[180] In another blow against accountability the NAMA legislation (section 56) contained an explicit gagging clause barring any criticism of government policy or of ministers by agency officials.[181] A subsequent announcement in March 2010 revealed that the composition of the private component of the SPV would be Irish Life Assurance (a part of the Irish Life & Permanent that has been at the centre of the Anglo deposits controversy and one of the most leveraged banks in the State), New Ireland (an insurance branch of Bank of Ireland), and AIB Investment Managers. In other words bankers were to be on both sides of the table negotiating the transfer of the loans. Conflict of interest? – you really couldn't make this up!

In addition to minimising political accountability the creation of the SPV primarily enabled the Government to keep the costs of NAMA off its official accounts. This had been aided by the European Commission's statistical service Eurostat accepting that NAMA would not be included in the figures used to calculate the national debt. The putative €54 billion required to

---

180 Nama is dead - we're on a special purpose vehicle, Sunday Business Post, 01/11/09.
181 Lenihan plans NAMA credit guidelines, RTE Business, 29/10/09.

fund NAMA represented around 30% of Gross Domestic Product (GDP). To include this in the national debt calculation, at a time when public debt was rising rapidly as a result of increased borrowing, would have pushed Ireland's debt/GDP ration well over 100%. Under the EU stability and growth pact, states are supposed to have a debt/GDP ratio of 60% or less. In late 2009 the Department of Finance estimated the Irish State's debt ratio at 59% rising to 73% by the end of 2010. This accounting sleight of hand, along with the period required to get its debt ratio down to targeted figures being extended, from two to five years[182] bought some time for the Irish Government and also, it was presumably hoped, for the credibility of the broader European project. However, it did not make the debt go away. It still had to be paid.

The most consistent claim made for NAMA was that it would restore the flow of credit and aid the revival of the economy. In an interview at the end of 2009 Brian Cowen confidently asserted that credit would flow again "when we take the distressed assets off the books of the banks."[183] The assumption was that once NAMA went live in early 2010 credit would be readily available to individuals and small businesses. Like many of the assumptions surrounding NAMA it is also completely baseless. Firstly, NAMA and the wider financial bailout depend upon a growing level of state borrowing, which will result in money flowing out of Ireland in the form of interest payments. Secondly, if the intention of NAMA was to get banks lending to small business and individuals again, why was Anglo Irish Bank included in the scheme? It does not have a retail branch network – and has no intention of establishing one – and was not a significant source of financing to small businesses. About half of its business was lending to middle–market companies and high net worth individuals, while the other 50 per cent comprised secured lending to property investors. Despite the lack of a small business focus, Anglo Irish will be the biggest beneficiary of NAMA.

---

182 NAMA won't be part of national debt, RTÉ Business, 20/10/09.

183 Facing down the toughest year in the life of Brian, Sunday Independent, December 27/12/09.

Thirdly there is the question of the NAMA bonds. It was originally suggested that the banks would use bonds given to them by NAMA to secure loans from the European Central Bank (ECB) and these funds would then be lent to Irish businesses and households.[184] In their public statements, ministers created the impression that NAMA was a clever mechanism for getting cheap European money flowing into Ireland. According to Minister John Gormley, NAMA was "about injecting a stimulus into the Irish economy through a very good deal with the ECB".[185] In fact there was no such deal: the ECB did not change its procedures to accommodate NAMA, nor did the NAMA legislation contain anything that required banks to borrow from the ECB and lend out those funds to Irish businesses.[186] This did not stop the "cheap ECB money" claim being made again and again. Examples of the gross distortion of the ECB's role in relation to NAMA included Fianna Fáil TD Seán Fleming telling RTÉ that "the taxpayer is not contributing any of this money . . . The European Central Bank is providing all the money";[187] and Minister Willie O'Dea informing listeners to RTÉ Radio One's Morning Ireland that "the ECB has agreed to give NAMA money."[188] In fact no such transactions will ever occur. The ECB will not be lending NAMA money at all. It is the Irish people who will contribute the money to pay for the NAMA assets and it is they who will have to pay.[189] The introduction of a "promissory note" to fund the first transfer of loans in March 2010 was also hailed as a master stroke but still meant that taxpayers were paying for the bail out.

There was no indication that the banks would use their NAMA funding to boost lending. In an appearance before a meeting of the Oireachtas Committee on Finance and the Public Sector in November 2009 bank executives were pressed on the issue of

---

184 Ireland's banks have delusion in their DNA, Sunday Independent, 20/12/09.

185 Gormley criticises Opposition plans, Irish Times, 11/09/09.

186 Nama will not put banks in position to lend more, Irish Times, 17/12/09.

187 RTE Six One News, 15/11/09.

188 RTÉ Radio One's Morning Ireland, 16/09/09.

189 NAMA From Heaven?, Irish Economy Blog, 16/09/09.

cashing the bonds with the ECB. CEOs Richie Boucher of Bank of Ireland (BoI) and Eugene Sheehy of Allied Irish Banks (AIB) pointedly refused to commit themselves to this. Indeed, the general tone of their statements was that there would be very little swapping of NAMA bonds for ECB loans. They also made it clear that the establishment of NAMA would not be a trigger for the flow of credit. Sheehy made that quite clear: "In regard to whether the banks will offer more money to a customer who enters one of our branches the day after NAMA is established, that will not happen."[190] Once again claims made for the agency did not correspond to how it would operate in practice. NAMA would not get credit flowing because this was not and has never been its purpose. Rather it was a mechanism for shoring up the crumbling banks and the bankers themselves made clear the naivety in assuming that this also meant reviving credit creation.

The failure to get credit flowing also makes it inevitable that there will be huge losses on the bad loans taken over by NAMA. In its projections the Government assumed that property prices had fallen by 40 per cent from their peak and that if prices rose by 10 per cent in the next decade (i.e. to 2004 levels) NAMA would break even. Given that the rise in property values was largely credit driven the only way that prices could return to 2004 levels was extraordinary economic growth or bank lending to grow at 2004 levels. But the continuing poor state of Irish banks, even after NAMA, makes this impossible.[191]

Zombie Banks

The Government promoted NAMA as a once and for all solution for the Irish banking system but it became clear that various forms of assistance to the banks would continue to be necessary after NAMA has been established. Not only did nationalisation of AIB seem inevitable but the progress of NAMA itself was

---

190 What Will the Banks Do with NAMA's Bonds?, Irish Economy Blog, 02/12/09.

191 Morgan Kelly – The Irish Credit Bubble – WP09/32, UCD Centre for Economic Research, December 2009.

painfully slow with the 'Financial Times' describing the whole process as "the slowest and most complex banking solution adopted around the world."[192] For apologists of the Government this was in fact a cunning plan, although perhaps only in the sense of the Baldrick character in the TV programme 'Blackadder'. Playing for time and waiting for something to turn up had more the flavour of that greater Irish creation, 'Waiting for Godot.'

The transfer of loans to NAMA was to begin in January 2010 but did not commence until the end of March. When they did, Brian Lenihan had to admit that the extent of the losses caused by "reckless" lending were "shocking." He announced that because of the losses on the loans being transferred to NAMA Anglo Irish would require not another €9 billion indicated by the new management of the bank but €8.3 billion and the possibility of another €10 billion on top of that. This would bring the total cost of saving the bank to over €22 billion and even then no one could have any confidence that it could then play any productive role thereafter. While claiming that the taxpayer's interests were "paramount" most of this money would simply disappear in covering the bank's horrendous losses. The sheer wastefulness was so appalling that Government spokesmen and especially Cowen went into scare mode, claiming that there was no other solution and on the Nine O'Clock News claiming that it would cost €100 billion to close the bank down.[193]

The new bail out was to be funded by promissory notes of €8.3 billion to Anglo and €2.6 billion to the Irish Nationwide Building Society (INBS). These would pay out €830 million and €260 million per year respectively for ten years starting in 2011, which meant taxpayers and their children would be paying over €1 billion until 2021 for something that was effectively already dead. Including the cost of an additional €10 billion in the bailout plus the cost of the State borrowing, the money to fund the payments would increase the annual cost to well over €2

---

192 Slow and Complex, Financial Times, 01/04/10.
193 Anglo: what are the options Irish Economy Blog, 03/04/10.

billion per year. This was approaching the level of cuts in public spending announced in the previous budget at the end of 2009. The cost of financing the national debt was already estimated at €4.6 billion for 2010.

The State would also be required to assist in the raising of an estimated €2.7 billion for Bank of Ireland and €7.4 billion for AIB. The real priority of the Government was to avoid State ownership of these two banks so it was believed that the investments already put into the banks, reflected in preference shares, would be converted into ordinary share capital. This would mean they went to the front in incurring losses and the taxpayer avoiding receipt of the eight per cent payment due on the preference the National Pension Reserve Fund which existed to fund the future pension entitlement of today's workers. The final element of this stunning business plan involved AIB selling off its most profitable foreign operations.shares. The balance might come from

Such were the losses involved in the rescue of Anglo that a debate immediately opened up on whether any other solution was possible. This focussed straight away on who should be compelled to pay for the mess and instantly revealed the class rules at play. Thus the banks could not afford to pay the interest on the preference shares invested by the State, supposedly on behalf of the taxpayer, so this was solved by turning the shares into a type of investment that had no automatic entitlement to a return but ranked first in taking losses. On the other hand the very idea of making other types of investors take a hit for their involvement in Anglo Irish was held as impossible, threatening the State itself with international pariah status and bankruptcy. This was the excuse behind the unwillingness of the Government to compel the estimated €2.4 billion invested by subordinated bondholders to suffer a loss, though their investment was a calculated risk. It also included €7.4 billion in senior debt which definitely could not be touched and, we were assured, ranked with depositors in terms of security, even if it too was a form of investment and in a not very well run, in fact "reckless", institution. Other liabilities included loans from the European Central Bank and other commercial banks but again banks were to be rescued no matter how badly run and no matter how stupid their investments had been. Deposits were also to be protected no matter their size, which especially in the case of Anglo, might have included large amounts that in effect were also investments. Only the taxpayer, totally unconnected to the banks, was to suffer loss. Of course shareholders had already lost out; including many older people relying on dividends from bank shares for their pension, but even the Government could not fully protect them. The identities of the losers were now well known but it became an increasing scandal that that of the winners was not.

The transfer of the toxic loans themselves produced much larger discounts to the face value than the 30 per cent predicted. The average turned out to be 47 per cent, with a high of 58 per cent for INBS and a low of 35 per cent for Bank of Ireland. This was held up as evidence of the protection given to the taxpayer but made more sense as a reflection of the even more disastrous character of the lending than had been assumed. It was clear that the checks on lending to rich developers were minimal to non–existent, with loans to developments that had not even received planning permission; or to developers who were buying from other people who never owned what they were selling; or on the basis of personal guarantees that were useless. The price of all this was to be paid in State bonds that would require annual interest payments and repayment of principal at the end. There was no updated NAMA business plan to pretend that a profit would be made out of all this. The assertion that interest receipts from the loans taken over would cover the interest payments generated from the additional State debt looked more and more incredible. Far from drawing a line under the bank rescue exercise the first transfer of loans only renewed speculation about how awful the reaming loans on the banks' books were and how much they might cost. Estimates of the total cost of the loans ranged from €45 billion to €50 billion with the grand total of the bail out being estimated by 'The Irish Times' as €82.875 billion.[194]

Other losses

It was not just the headline losses on the loans transferred to NAMA that illustrated the continuing weakness of the banks. The collapse of the property bubble and general economic contraction affected banking activity across the board. According to international debt rating agency Moody's this will continue to lead to "very substantial arrears and losses" for the Irish banks. Their profitability was also "likely to reduce as a result of lower volumes and the higher costs of wholesale and retail funding." While the ratings of Irish banks had not changed their losses were having a negative impact on their capital base. This was only offset by the Government's commitment to "providing further capital to the sector if required," which for some institutions was the "only potential source of capital."[195] Finance Minister Brian Lenihan repeatedly pledged that the Government would be the capital provider of last resort if the banks failed to raise the necessary money elsewhere. One of the consequences of this is that in the space of two years the three main Irish-owned banks will have gone from private ownership to some form of state ownership, whether that is full nationalisation or the Government taking a majority shareholding. This would serve to illustrate that there is nothing inherently progressive about state ownership. In the case of the Irish banks, where it has been a mechanism for the transfer of wealth from the working majority to the capitalist class, it has been completely reactionary.

Even if the claims made for NAMA were accepted it could never be a once and for all solution to the Irish banking crisis. This is because it addresses only one part of that crisis when the problems facing the banks are actually threefold. Firstly, they have suffered large losses on developer loans. Secondly, to fund

---

194 Is your head spinning from bank numbers? Let's try again, Irish Times, 03/04/10.

195 Irish banks face 'very substantial arrears and losses', warns debt rating agency, Irish Times, 16/12/09.

sharply increased lending they have borrowed heavily in wholesale markets. Thirdly, losses on other loans, in particular mortgages, are likely to be substantial. NAMA is designed to address the first problem of developer loans but it does not address the other two: the liabilities associated with large wholesale debt and further losses on other loans.

In 2009, AIB had outstanding bonds of €24 billion (plus €5 billion subordinated debt) and ECB borrowings of €34 billion. Bank of Ireland had bonds of €45 billion (plus €8 billion subordinated) and ECB borrowing of €17 billion. This is well beyond the value of the bonds (€17 billion for AIB and €11 billion for the BoI) that the banks were at that time forecast to receive from NAMA. Also, their position will become more difficult with the withdrawal of ECB support. During the period of the international financial crisis Irish banks benefited from the ECB's policy of quantitative easing. With the big Eurozone economies moving out of recession that lending facility will be curtailed. Domestic deposits as a source of capital have also come under pressure as the Irish economy contracted. In the year to September 2009 deposits from Irish residents had fallen by 5.5 per cent.

The banks also face the prospect of further loans losses, particularly on mortgages. A fall in house prices alongside a dramatic rise in unemployment would see mortgage defaults increase. A figure for Ireland has not been reported but the situation in the US, with a similar combination of factors, produced mortgage default rates of 15 per cent. Given the level of unemployment an even higher default rate could not be excluded in Ireland. Predictions of the effect this might have in the Irish State included a forecast that for AIB it would take a loss of 16 per cent on its mortgage book of €33 billion (to wipe out a post–NAMA book capital of €5 billion) and that it would only take a loss of 5 per cent on Bank of Ireland's much larger mortgage book of €59 billion to seriously damage its post-NAMA book capital.[196] While not all the assets and liabilities associated with the Irish banking system are bad, their

---

196 Kelly, December 2009.

enormous size means that even a modest fall in the value of assets, an increase in the cost of borrowing or rate of loan default, could incur a substantial loss for the State.

Summary

NAMA, and the broader financial bailout of which it is part, is a mechanism to rescue the bankers and the property developers. Many of the claims made for it and the assumptions which underpin its projections are false. It is not a once and for all solution to the banking crisis; it will not turn on the flow of credit or help revive the economy. NAMA will not break even, let alone return a modest profit to the public purse. Its nature as a bailout means that the banks must benefit and the public incur a loss, either through tax receipts invested or exorbitant cost for banking services. The value of the losses incurred by NAMA cannot yet be calculated, but on the basis of what we do know about the state of the loans taken on it will be substantial. Taken together with the other costs associated with the bailout the total cost could be beyond the financial capacity of the state. The bank bailout could push the Irish State towards bankruptcy, opening up the possibility of institutions such as the EU and the IMF intervening to impose a solution – the very scenario that the Government claims it is trying to avoid.

In a sense NAMA is irrational – it cannot succeed and may actually produce the opposite of what it is supposed to achieve. This is the substance of the criticisms from the academic economists who have been the most vocal mainstream opposition to NAMA.[197] They base their arguments on a theoretical view of capitalism in which people who make bad investments, such and bankers and property developers, take a loss and go out of business. The financial bailout is an affront to this, but is closer to how capitalism actually operates in practice, reflecting the reality of class interest and class rule.

At its heart NAMA is a mechanism of class rule – a means to transfer wealth from labour to capital and make workers pay for

---

197 Nama set to shift wealth to lenders and developers, Irish Times, 26/08/09.

a crisis created by the capitalist class and its system. Public and private sector workers are paying through job cuts, wage reductions and deteriorating working conditions while the broader working class faces poorer public services, higher charges and reduced benefits. There is a direct transfer of funding from public services into the banks. NAMA and the broader financial bailout threaten to burden the Irish working class for a generation. There are no possible reforms to how it might work that could make it in any way a progressive measure.

Chapter 3

'A Better, Fairer Way?'

"We believe there is a better, fairer way to tackle this crisis, one that doesn't place the entire burden on low and middle income earners, one that gets people back to work and that doesn't crash the economy completely."

This is some text from a leaflet printed by the Irish Congress of Trade Unions before a number of demonstrations on November 6, 2009, called to demand an alternative economic course by the Government, and in support of ICTU's 'Ten Point Plan for National Recovery.' The question that therefore presents itself is, is ICTU's ten point plan an alternative? From the text of the leaflet quoted there is cause for doubt. What does it mean when it says that the "entire" burden should not fall on low and middle income earners? What does it mean when it says ICTU's way will not crash the economy "completely"? How much less than completely is being proposed?

It is our view that the Congress plan does not represent an alternative that can be supported. Since workers did not create the economic crisis their fair share of the pain in paying for it should be zero. But ICTU doesn't accept this. It believes that working people have to accept some of the burden – a fair share of the burden. Its policy is based on this even while it admits that "lower and middle income earners – much less those on social welfare – played no role in causing this crisis."[198] So how

---

198 Congress Ten Point Plan for a Better fairer way, pages 10–11.

much workers should pay remains a mystery; while ICTU insists a fair share must be paid, it nowhere explains how much pain it would be fair for working people to bear.

Responsibility

It has become fashionable to claim that we all bear some responsibility for the mess or must all make a contribution to putting things right. But how much sense does it make to say we all contributed to the mess, and how are we all making a contribution when these contributions flow in only one direction, from workers to the banks? At the start of the boom there was a real pent–up demand for housing. It was entirely understandable that many took the opportunity to buy their own homes. Public provision of housing has always been woeful and the Government's weak initiatives to increase it during the boom were totally inadequate. The only option for most was to buy their own home, and in a situation of rapidly rising prices the incentive was to buy as quickly as possible before prices put even the most modest houses out of reach. This was indeed what happened and many became priced out of the market or worse – over-extended themselves in getting their first or next foot on the property ladder.

The argument for blaming everyone for the property bubble is that some responded to the incentives in place to buy bigger homes or even a second home. Many of these individuals are now in twice as much trouble as a result. But what were such people doing except responding to the incentives put in place by the existing economic system? Were these incentives not those that all the economic experts and commentators extolled as the basis of a dynamic and prosperous society? Is it not the case that these incentives all pointed disastrously in the wrong direction and that this is the fault of the system that created them, not those who did what they were told, thinking that they had found a relatively easy way to wealth and security.

It has been ironic that a system and its supporters which condemned rising costs and declared support for incentives to hard work has found itself manufacturing a bubble consisting of rapidly rising house prices which promised income and wealth involving next to no work at all. But this does not make working people responsible for this situation. Those who were able took advantage of what they thought was a means of securing their future through investing in property, while others simply got on the property ladder as quickly as possible before it became impossible. They did so in response to advice from almost all the financial and economic experts and in response to the clear advice and tax incentives provided by the Government.

Workers, unlike developers or speculators, had no Chief Financial Officer, with professional knowledge and numerous professional advisors, to help them determine what to do, or to allow them to get the best deal with the banks. Now that the bubble has burst they now have no NAMA to bail them out and no means of writing off losses against future taxes. The finance industry took the opportunity of increasing privatisation of basic public services to make money out of workers who have had no choice but avail of its services. Not only housing but education (most obviously at third level), pensions and health services are all increasingly available only through the financial services industry, either through loans, insurance or savings products. During the boom these payments funded obscene bank bonuses and profits. Now 'pension levies' and increased taxes are helping to pay for the bankers' bailouts so that they can once again be made profitable and once again return to the bonus culture. Just like that earlier experiment in popular capitalism, Eircom, workers have paid dearly. Some, such as those in Waterford Glass, have found that after years of paying pension contributions there is nothing there when they need it. Their money has simply disappeared – into past years fees, commissions and charges and into the stock market crash. Far from being accomplices in the great property bubble, workers have all along been its victims; no more so than now, when the whole thing has crashed down to earth.

The argument that workers must pay their 'fair' share therefore rests on the idea that we are all in this together. We all gained something from the boom and all must now pay something in the bust. But this too does not bear serious examination.

Wages and employment did indeed rise but this is only one side of the story. The boom resulted in the cost of living soaring in the Irish State with stores like Tesco making their highest profits in Ireland. Above all the share of national income going to workers declined over the boom while that going to profits increased. We did not all share equally in the boom and in fact there was no call from those now demanding a shared pain that we did so. Banks lending to workers didn't care if they could afford to pay their mortgages. If they couldn't pay them, well many were securitised anyway, and they could simply be evicted and someone else brought in. Rising prices could ensure that money could be made selling the houses that existing occupiers could no longer afford to buy. Now we are told that we are all in this together, although it is clear that we are not.

In September 2008, the heads of the Irish banks got a pledge from the Government that the State would guarantee all the banks' debts – over €440 thousand million, over twice GDP, and a sum of money that could not possibly be afforded. Would anyone else get such a deal? It was described by Brian Lenihan as the cheapest bank bailout in the world, but it was anything but. In 2009 €11 billion was committed to recapitalising the insolvent banks, including the nationalisation of Anglo Irish, which made taxpayers responsible for its huge losses and debt. This bank was run as a private money collecting machine for the well–connected to use in enormous property speculation. It was and is wholly useless and is now insolvent, yet the Government used taxpayers' money to protect those bond holders who invested in it. All this is being paid for by cutting wages, social welfare and public services. The cuts are justified by the need to reduce the budget deficit but then this deficit explodes to pay for NAMA. Around €54 thousand million was initially to be borrowed to bail out the banks on top of that already given by way of recapitalisation. But even before it was up and running it was clear that NAMA would not save the banks and Davy Research, in a report on the Irish banks in July 2009, estimated that the total recapitalisation would cost between €20 and €25 billion.[199] This proved to be a gross

---

199 Government finances and banks, Davy Research, July 2009, page 3.

underestimate. The State has said it will pay whatever it costs – through taxes on working people and cuts in public services that will impact for years and years ahead. What is involved is a massive transfer of wealth from the poor to the very rich. The idea that we are all in this together is fanciful.

Once it is accepted that working people either bear some portion of the blame for the crisis, or have some responsibility to pay for it, the question becomes one of merely haggling over the amount. Once it is accepted that there should be no fundamental challenge to the existing economic system, and its prioritisation of the profits of those who own capital, especially the banks, sacrifices by workers for the sake of those much wealthier are simply inevitable. What we are left with
then is a better and fairer way, courtesy of ICTU, that is neither better nor fairer.

Ten Point Plan

The fundamental problem with this "better and fairer way" is that while Congress sometimes speaks of the economic crisis as a "crisis of global capitalism" it does not seek an anti–capitalist alternative.[200] At most it complains of liberal policies or the neo–classical approach to economics. It does not reject the logic of the existing capitalist system but thinks that by looking at it in a different way alternative policies can be found. Its ten point plan is striking evidence that the restrictions on constructing an alternative while accepting the fundamentals of the system are overwhelming. Congress however believes that such an alternative already exists. In the context of the banking crisis it calls for the Government to move away from the "Anglo–American Shareholder value model to a more inclusive European–style stakeholder interest model."[201] The evidence that there is a capitalism in Europe or Japan fundamentally better and fairer than the one existing in Ireland does not withstand examination. Banks in Germany, Austria, Belgium

---

200 Congress Ten Point Plan for a Better fairer way, page 14.
201 Congress Ten Point Plan for a Better fairer way, page 16.

and across Eastern Europe have all had to be bailed out. In April 2009 The EU Commission reported that €3 trillion had been paid out in bank bailouts, while the fallout from a property bubble in Japan has now lasted two decades. The 'Financial Times' columnist Martin Wolff noted at the beginning of January 2010 that "the peak to trough decline of the US economy was only 3.8 per cent . . . while the eurozone's was 5.1 per cent."[202]

The core argument of Congress is not that the crisis can be solved differently from the way pursued by the Government but that the time over which it is implemented should be longer – "elongating our adjustment period until 2017."[203] Congress points to the example of Britain, where its former new Labour Government introduced stimulus measures and postponed public spending cuts. It also pins its hopes on the Irish Government's fanciful claims that growth will return to 4 per cent to 5 per cent in a few years so allowing the State's debt levels to reduce "with some relative ease."[204] This scenario ignores the fact that the Irish State has de–facto had a stimulus in place ever since tax revenues dependent on the property bubble collapsed while at the same time spending was maintained or fell more slowly. All the cuts implemented in 2008 and 2009 have only been designed to stabilise the budget deficit at around 12 per cent. None of this stimulus prevented the fastest contracting economy in the developed world during 2009 from shrinking or unemployment rising by nearly 45 per cent, even while immigrants have left and many Irish–born have left the labour force.

The Irish State cannot print money in imitation of Britain's policy of quantitative easing because it does not have its own currency and is nowhere near powerful enough even if it did. Congress bemoans as "highly unrealistic and potentially catastrophic" the policy of cutting the Government's deficit to 3 per cent of Gross Domestic Product by 2013, but this is a target set by the EU and it is ironic that Congress fully supported the

202 Why the eurozone has a tough decade to come, Martin Wolff, Financial Times 6 January 2010.
203 Ibid, page 6.
204 Ibid, page 5.

EU and its liberal, neo–classical policies when avidly endorsing ratification of the Lisbon Treaty.[205]   Congress argues that cutting the budget deficit is possible over a longer period and that this can be done with the full agreement of the EU and the international financial markets. That is, the same EU and capital markets that are the real driving forces behind the demand for existing catastrophic cuts.

The trade unions' deference, and that of the Government and Irish State, to the powerful economic and political forces that currently determines its policy reflects the fact that the Irish State is still an outpost of an empire, though one no longer controlled solely by Britain. Hoping to do the bidding of these forces while protecting Irish workers is impossible. The EU and international capital will not accept postponing cuts in Irish living standards and it makes no sense to ask their permission to take longer to do it. The most Congress policy would achieve is more borrowing leading to a larger debt at a higher cost in interest payments resulting in bigger cuts thereafter.

International capital has already expressed anxiety that the Irish State faces insolvency, unease motivated by concern over the money it is owed and the threat to the euro rather than concern over the rapid damage inflicted on Irish society. Congress claims that the level of State debt is manageable but then adds "provided NAMA works."[206]   Indeed, even then Congress has to acknowledge that NAMA enormously extends the level of debt that will have to be paid back with interest. While it ignores all evidence and argument that NAMA will not work this admission alone destroys its macroeconomic perspective of increasing debt to boost recovery.

While the core argument of ICTU that the pain must be elongated is not an alternative, its policy on NAMA is one of abject surrender. Congress does not oppose this massive transfer of wealth to those so deeply implicated in causing the crisis but peddles the most absurd illusions that it can be made

---

205 Ibid, page 4.
206 Congress Ten Point Plan for a Better fairer way, page 6.

to have some progressive content. While recording that "Congress has serious misgivings about the NAMA legislation", and acknowledging that the "bank bail out is the biggest public expenditure risk on behalf of taxpayers ever undertaken in the history of the Irish state" Congress nevertheless declares that "as NAMA is the chosen methodology of Government, Congress will critically support it in the national interest."[207] Congress states that this support is conditional on a "social dividend" component to NAMA but it is clear to everyone that the purpose of NAMA is to save the banks not to fund "[more?] housing, schools, health centres, sports and other community facilities."[208] ICTU's critical and conditional support has been covered by an excuse that NAMA involves a political decision and ICTU has no place taking political stances that challenge the Government. If this were really so then ICTU would really have no reason for putting forward any proposals at all, except in so far as they are simply appeals to the better nature, or a second thought, from a Government that has shown no sign of either.

It is clear however that it is not only the Government that doesn't pause for reflection. ICTU proposes a "National Recovery Bond to fund specific infrastructural projects with the objective of meeting a national need and providing construction employment."[209] One problem with this concept is that it is in direct competition for funding with the banks that the Government is so desperately trying to save, and with Congress support. The suggestion that this initiative could "be done off balance sheet" is a staggeringly stupid repeat of the same financial shenanigans which helped create the crisis in the first place and which is being repeated with NAMA.[210] There seems no earthly reason why workers should support the Government and construction industry continuing to spend millions of their taxes on infrastructure when the mess we are in is in no small part the result of this partnership doing exactly this. There could be no guarantee that the same corruption would not

207 Ibid, page 15 and There is still a Better, Fairer Way: 2010 Pre–Budget Submission, ICTU 2009, page 29.

208 There is still a Better, Fairer Way: 2010 Pre–Budget Submission, ICTU 2009, page 30.

209 Congress Ten Point Plan for a Better fairer way, page 8.

210 Ibid, page 8.

simply be given one more opportunity to blossom. In any case the NAMA business plan envisages taxpayers continuing to fund the great property speculation through providing developers with €5 billion or more to complete their developments. As this will no doubt involve additional construction employment it appears that ICTU's alternative is once again not so alternative after all.

This is equally the case for Congress's favoured plan to rescue the banks, which is to nationalise them. This proposal in the past might have seemed quite radical and in some sense it was, but now it is by no means progressive. The nationalisation of the crony bank Anglo–Irish is evidence of this. It maintains a useless bank in existence which has devoured taxpayers money in keeping it half afloat, has done nothing to generate renewed investment in productive enterprise, which it never did anyway, and Government control has so far successfully hidden its very guilty secrets. That nationalisation per se is no radical measure which workers should support is at least indicated by the approval of such a measure by the IMF and OECD, both notoriously right wing institutions. That these bodies see it as a purely temporary measure does not make its permanence progressive.

Nationalisation is a more direct and possibly more effective means of working people saving these institutions and taking the burden of property speculators' losses on to themselves. Opponents of nationalisation have argued that it leads to political interference and inevitable corruption. That this has already been true of the existing privately owned system should blind no one to the truth of the charge. It is also however completely true of NAMA, which is simply, after all, a 'bad bank.' Supporters of nationalisation argue that it at least gives taxpayers the chance of an upside if the banks go back to profitability, especially if the bad loans are taken from them through NAMA. This proposal however still requires workers to pay for the bad debts and assumes that even after the developers' loans have been taken away the losses on ordinary mortgage and business debt will not also bankrupt these organisations all over again, with workers in line to pay again.

It takes only a moment to realise that proposals for a banking system run by a Government that has shown itself so incompetent, dishonest and corrupt can not be seen as progressive. Anglo Irish demonstrates that it does not even save the jobs of the ordinary workers employed in the banks. The appeals to nationalise, which have come not just from Congress, have been vehemently rejected by the Government and its supporters, even after Anglo was taken over. The obvious ideological element to this opposition might again be ditched if NAMA fails to save the banks and the Government is compelled to directly take them over. If so, this would not represent a victory for working people.

Not all of Congress's proposals have been rejected outright. Their suggestion of a recovery bond did receive some sort of validation with the Government announcing a 'national solidarity bond' for small investors. This, however, hardly merited a mention in reports of the December 2009 budget and was more or less ignored. Like its proposal for a €1 billion fund to retain jobs, the proposal is too small for the task at hand. Moreover, these initiatives involve subsidising private capital, exclude worker involvement in controlling the spending of their tax money and rest on the dubious ground that the expenditure will help solve what Congress views mainly as a "demand" crisis. This view is that the worldwide recession has been sparked off by a severe contraction in credit (following its unsustainable extension) but ignores the reality that the worldwide extension of credit and debt could not continue indefinitely. It was bound to stop growing, and when it did a severe contraction was equally bound to result.

The policy of the biggest powers has been to attempt to replace private sector debt that has been exposed to losses with direct and indirect subsidies that simply replaces it with public sector debt. In the longer term, and not so long term, this too is unsustainable. Workers in these countries are already being called upon to pay the price of repaying the mountains of debt created, either through cuts in services, wages and tax increases or through a renewed bout of inflation. This may result in a dynamic of deleveraging and recession that we see in evidence in Ireland today. The Ten Point Plan of ICTU only amounts to postponing the day of reckoning. This day will be quicker and harder for the least powerful states and companies, amongst whom must be included Ireland Inc. This is all the more so because the Irish crisis cannot be understood as simply a crisis of demand, as ICTU maintains. Both the construction and financial services industries became oversized, certainly as a result of the massive increase in credit, but also because their growth was profitable and, at least in the case of construction, initially necessary. As we have noted housing grew from four to six per cent of national income in the 1990s to 15 per cent at the height of the boom.[211] That a speculative frenzy developed is as much due to the unplanned and profit-driven nature of the economic system as an exaggerated expansion of credit and lax to non–existent regulation.

"There will be no return to business as usual", "everything must change" says Congress.[212] Yet nowhere is it proposed how this will happen. Appeals are made to a Government that has shown itself irredeemably rotten. Fianna Fail holds the very people who led the headlong charge into the crisis. For most people it is impossible to think of the economic disaster without thinking of them. The Green Party has shown a unique combination of devotion to the trappings of power, plus terror of losing it, and the most light-headed belief in their own mission to save the planet. Sincere stupidity prevents many of them from doing the only thing they really could do to help, which is to call a halt to the wrecking of peoples lives in this one small part of the planet. Fine Gael have made clear again and again to anyone who cares to listen that they support saving the banks and making the cuts necessary to grant international capital its debt repayment and interest. The Labour Party has presented the appearance of opposition while also making it clear that no point of principle stands in its way in forming a coalition with Fine Gael in order to do essentially what Fianna Fail is doing. Their objection is purely that Fianna Fail is guilty of making it necessary in the first place, although their own policies would have made little

---

211 'The Irish Credit Bubble', Morgan Kelly, UCD WP09/32, December 2009, page 1.

212 Congress Ten Point Plan for a Better fairer way', pages 2 and 16.

difference. It is clear that none of the existing parties support Congress's plan yet the obvious conclusion is not stated – that workers need their own party. Were Congress serious even about its own professed policies the construction of a new party to fight for them would at least be the subject of open debate and argument. That it is not so is because the ten point plan is not a plan at all. It is a protest. A cry of 'not in our name' which declares that we are opposed to this and are not part of it but that we are not going to fight to stop it or put something in its place.

ICTU

The better and fairer way of Congress's Ten Point Plan thus leads not to a fight for an alternative but to a capitulation to the policies of the Government. This is signalled in the plan itself through its appeal simply to postpone "adjustment", itself a weasel word of the right, and its acceptance of "wage moderation".[213] It readily explains the behaviour of ICTU throughout the crisis and the repeated pronouncements of trade union leaders revealing their innocence of opposition. At the end of November 2009 Jack O'Connor of SIPTU commenced negotiations with the Government by claiming that pay had risen "disproportionately" during the boom and must be readjusted. At the start of that month Peter McLoone agreed that ICTU's plans involved "a significant reduction in public service numbers over the next three to four years" with additional measures on top of these. A day later Blair Horan of the Civil Public and Services Union said that job losses were "inevitable." The day after one quarter of a million public sector workers went on strike to defend their livelihoods Peter McLoone of IMPACT agreed that payroll costs should be cut.[214] The eventual offer by ICTU of 12 days unpaid leave was ultimately rejected by the Government but ICTU had already by then surrendered every principle up for negotiation by also

213 Ibid, pages 6 and 11.

214 Union leader says 'pay rose too much in boom', The Irish Times, 29 November, 2009. Public sector union leader says holding pay means jobs go, The Irish Times, 3 November, 2009. Group says pay threats will not be tolerated, The Irish Times, 4 November, 2009. Public sector unions agree payroll costs must be cut next year, The Irish Times, 25 November, 2009.

agreeing to dramatic changes to public sector terms and conditions of employment. In March 2010, it accepted this plan, which it had vehemently declared was withdrawn, in return for Government pledges that it might not make any more public sector pay cuts. ICTU signalled a definitive surrender by promising not to engage in any industrial action while public services were decimated as part of the deal.

Thus ICTU has not only failed to provide an alternative in a policy sense, on the level of a programme to which their members and others could subscribe, they have also failed at a practical level to prevent or even reduce the attacks. With each assault ICTU signalled its acceptance by holding up some other issue as the one on which it would fight, only to meekly surrender on this as well. The only successful opposition to cuts as these lines have been written has come from the elderly, opposing the attempt to take away automatic entitlement to a medical card, and it is instructive that they are not organised by ICTU. So, given the lack of a real alternative during the crisis, an obvious question arises. To what extent did Congress offer an alternative to the policies that contributed so much to the crisis in the first place? To put it more directly – to what extent is Congress also responsible?

ICTU is acutely aware that fingers are pointed at it, that it "must share in the blame for the bust".[215] Its answer is that Congress was in social partnership but not in Government. While it seeks to take some credit for the 'good' boom it takes no responsibility for the 'bad' boom, while still claiming that it "mitigated the liberal economic policies of deregulation, privatisation and tax-cutting, which ultimately led to the collapse of the Irish economy in 2008."[216] It is tempting to ask just how bad Congress is claiming the bust would have been had it not "mitigated" Government policy. This defensive reaction is perfectly understandable and entirely warranted. Even now, by its own words, it continues to justify having been partners with a Government and employer class while these fashioned the

---

215 There is still a Better, Fairer Way: 2010 Pre–Budget Submission, ICTU 2009, page 4.
216 Ibid, page 5.

conditions that resulted in the current disaster. It might be tempting for Congress to claim that it is only now that we are seeing both the greed and corruption of its partners and the devastation facilitated by their policies. This however would not have a shred of credibility. The corruption at the heart of the Irish State and business class was in evidence years ago and was reported widely and repeatedly year after year. The potentially disastrous nature of the economic policies pursued was also criticised year after year but on not one occasion did Congress seriously threaten to stop being partners with these people. Even now it seeks desperately to find some way of maintaining partnership. With partnership comes responsibility and Congress bears its "fair" share. There is no point claiming it did not make policy. Its claims for social partnership were precisely that it allowed ICTU to influence policy beyond mere pay and conditions. Either it did or it didn't and either way ICTU is condemned.

Their responsibility for the crisis goes further than failing to fight it, failing to offer an alternative to it and being partners with those whose policies and system created it. Their responsibility is in many cases a personal one. It is barely possible to read ICTU statements condemning the corporate governance of Irish business without recalling that Peter McLoone of IMPACT was chairman of the state agency FAS during the time when its corporate governance was almost as rotten as that of the banks. He was not alone. FAS was stuffed with Congress sponsored directors. It is simply impossible to take seriously Congress damnation of financial regulation when its General Secretary has been on the board of the Central Bank, with ultimate responsibility for regulation, since 1995. He was even chair of its audit committee. It is equally absurd to take at face value ICTU's professed opposition to privatisation while worker representatives sat on the board of Aer Lingus with now disgraced Anglo Irish banker Sean Fitzpatrick. What these and many other examples demonstrate is that social partnership is very real but it is not at all of the nature portrayed by the social partners themselves. Working people do not sit on the boards of banks or state agencies with the captains of Irish business. Ordinary workers are not in partnership with their bosses, not now and not ever. The real partnership process involves the trade union bureaucrats of Congress and no one else.

When 'The Irish Times' ran a series of stories exposing the huge salaries and perks enjoyed by top trade union functionaries many saw it as a thinly disguised attack on the whole trade union movement. While this is obviously the motivation behind the stories such a defence ignores one rather obvious fact. The stories are true. It is true that trade union bureaucrats earn multiples of their members; that David Begg has an annual income in excess of €160,000 plus company car; that Jack O'Connor of SIPTU gets nearly €125,000, John Carr of the teachers' union INTO over €170,000, Blair Horan of the low paid civil servants union €120,000 etc. etc. The only thing that puts several other union leaders even further out of touch with the living conditions of their members is that they refused to disclose how much they were paid. Imagine if Brian Cowen or Brian Lenihan attempted that! It is not a question of individual corruption. It is worse than this.

The leadership of the trade union movement is a whole social layer, a bureaucracy, with obvious and immediate conditions of life radically different from the members they are supposed to represent. This is most starkly demonstrated by their salaries and by their appointment to state bodies, with the status and prestige that goes with it. It is less obvious but no less pernicious when these people leave trade union employment and go on to lucrative positions on the boards of yet more state sponsored bodies. Their salaries may be dependent on workers' union subscriptions but the state facilitates the collection of these subscriptions and it is no accident that Congress has more and more become an organisation dependent on state employment for its membership. Trade union leaders are thus dependent on the state for their relatively privileged position. This is not a cynical argument. It is a fact. The failure of Congress to fight for their members has its foundation in their relatively privileged and secure position which depends as much, if not more, on not challenging the government as it does on their union membership. The current economic and political system does not, is not, threatening them as it is their members.

It is unnecessary to look any further for an explanation for ICTU's failures.

Social partnership between workers and the State plus the bosses is therefore a myth, but partnership between the trade union leadership and the State and business class is an obvious reality. Working people have therefore no stake in partnership for they aren't part of it. During the boom they traded increased wages for lower taxes that necessitated rotten public services, so that even during the height of the boom cancer sufferers were dying on a waiting list while money bought life. The boom created employment but it could not create security. It delivered higher wages but also an exorbitant cost of living. Congress traded on delivering the sort of pay rises that any economic boom would have delivered of itself through a tight labour market. Now it is responsible for failing to protect workers during the crisis and failing at every level to offer an alternative. Through social partnership it collaborated with the forces that led to the Irish economic disaster and has failed to advance a political alternative. To now respond to the crisis, to offer an alternative, it is necessary to put forward a political alternative.

Through social partnership ICTU has demonstrated that its politics are fundamentally the same as those who benefited most from the boom and are now getting everyone else to pay for the bust. Congress's biggest failure is that it has stood against Irish workers developing their own political alternative, for that is what is now needed. Such an alternative has almost nothing in common with its Ten Point Plan or its "better, fairer way."

Chapter 4

The Alternative: A Manifesto for Resistance

"You found that your view of the world, your ideology, was not right – it was not working?"

This was the question asked by a US House of Representatives' Chairman on October 2008 to the former Chairman of the Federal Reserve, Alan Greenspan. Greenspan had for years been hailed by the world's financial markets as something of a mastermind who had allowed free market capitalism to deliver boom and prosperity year after year. Greenspan's answer was nothing if not honest – 'Absolutely, precisely. You know, that's precisely the reason I was shocked, because I have been going for forty years or more with very considerable evidence that it was working exceptionally well.'[217] Now the evidence says something very different.

The evidence has been of an economic crisis which, at one point, appeared on the verge of creating complete economic collapse. Having survived this through huge state intervention a promise of recovery has been offered, but only if we accept higher unemployment and huge cuts in living standards. In Ireland we have had a boom that delivered an enormous crisis and are promised a recovery that promises years of misery. Even the most naive would pause to think, surely there is an alternative to all this? Yet that is precisely what we are told does not exist. And who tells us this? Why the same people, like Greenspan, who were shocked that capitalism had once again delivered an almighty collapse.

---

217 'Meltdown: the end of the age of greed', Paul Mason, page 118, London 2009, Verso.

Of course the crisis answers one thing very clearly: it is not a question of whether an alternative is necessary but what sort of alternative is required. The financial and business press in 2009 and 2010 has been frantically warning that we cannot continue in the same way as before. The definition of insanity is doing the same thing again and again and expecting a different result. Pundits worldwide identify the next possible bubble and fear the state is all out of ammunition to fight it. Yet what is striking is that there is no agreement even among those who believe there is no alternative on what should now be done. Having been told that only stagnation could result from regulated capitalism we are now told that free market capitalism threatens uncontrollable instability.

The truth is that the economic system cannot be controlled; indeed its unrestrained character is the essential nature of its existence. Control and planning is precisely what the defenders of capitalism claim cannot be achieved because that is called socialism. The defenders of capitalism are therefore in the end correct, there is no alternative within capitalism to the possibility, indeed inevitability, of crisis. Economic crisis is precisely the mechanism by which the tensions and contradictions within the economic system are resolved, and resolved at the expense of those capitalists forced into bankruptcy and the wider working population forced to pick up the bill required to restore growth to those capitalists surviving. What this means is that if one is looking for an alternative to the massive cuts in living standards now demanded, the obscene transfer of wealth from the poorest to the very richest, and with no promise that a renewed crisis will not erupt, in fact the very opposite, then one has to look beyond capitalism.

All this is no less true of Ireland which, more than most, has worshipped at the shrine of unbridled capitalism. That is why the crisis is so much worse here. It is why the cuts in living standards are so much more severe and why the prospect is of years of austerity and misery that stretch indefinitely into the future. It is why the Government, economic experts and bankers expressed such confidence in a bubble economy, why they were in denial even as it burst and why they expressed such shock when it hit them in the face. To hear them now tell us that there is no alternative to their policies and their system is to invite ridicule. More important, it is time to construct an alternative, both on paper and in action.

That the problem is one of the system explains why those so obviously guilty are the beneficiaries of all attempts to clean up the mess. The Government is wedded to the bankers and property speculators, but these are also the people who own and control the economic system. Saving it means saving the people who own it and run it. That is why bankers and all the actors complicit in the bubble economy have been called in to help run NAMA. It is not enough to blame them or the corrupt politicians for we cannot rid ourselves of them without breaking with their system.

That is why none of the proposals, not only from the Government, but from the Dail opposition parties, can guarantee that it will not all happen again, because they too are partisans of the existing system. Fine Gael recognises that saving broken institutions from bankruptcy will not make them lend or contribute to a growing economy. They do however agree with the Government that workers should help pay for the rotten loans and they have proposed more draconian cuts than Fianna Fail and the Greens. Nationalisation, put forward by many, including the Labour Party, would still mean that tax payers, overwhelmingly workers, would foot the bill. It is not a socialist measure and nationalisation of Anglo Irish has been seen correctly by every serious commentator as a bailout of the bankers and developers involved. Like nearly all the voices calling for nationalisation, the Labour Party want to sell the banks back to private owners after workers have paid to clean them up. Even those who have supported it are rightly fearful of the cronyism that would immediately infect state ownership and control. Rather than being an alternative, creeping state ownership has become the inevitable consequence of current Government policy.

It was revealed in 2009 that perhaps one third of the state bonds issued by the Government to pay for its debt had been bought by the same banks that the Government was bailing out. The banks gave money to the state for bonds and the state gave the money to the banks to bail them out! The banks were supposed to use the bonds they had bought to get cash from the European Central Bank to lend to small business and workers, but why do this when easier and less risky profits are available? The whole Irish banking system had become one giant pyramid scheme, one that workers pay for. Drastic cuts leading to unemployment and fear for the future are presented as means to instil confidence and promote recovery!

These are examples of the policies that are intended to make the working majority pay for the crisis and the point of this short book is to give working people an alternative, a set of demands and policies to fight for which defends their interests and makes those responsible for the crisis pay for it. The Irish working class therefore needs to mobilise around a set of demands that can offer a defence of their living standards and which brings into view some alternatives to what is being put forward by the current political consensus.

The priority is to develop an independent outlook at both an economic and political level. It is essential that the working class has its own policy, its own programme, and the organisations to fight for it. What is set out below is a set of demands that could provide the basis for such a movement. These demands not only address the immediate concerns of workers but also point towards the socialist transformation of society. Their immediate objective is to strengthen the organisations of working people through defensive activities and rebuilding solidarity. The demands are not some sort of wish list, or a con trick to demonstrate the bankruptcy of the Government (for many people that is already evident). They are put forward as practical solutions that, if taken on board by a broad movement, can at the very least mitigate the impact of the crisis on working people, and at best begin the transformation of Irish society. The outcome of the crisis is not predetermined but dependent on a class struggle that will develop over the coming years both in Ireland and across the world. As Greenspan admitted, his ideology, and that of corporate and political Ireland has failed. It is time for an alternative.

General Election Now!

The most remarkable aspect of the crisis is not the jaw–dropping lines in the graphs showing falling house prices and production, or rising lines recording unemployment and State debt. The most astounding fact is that after over eighteen months of staggering crisis the Government that did so much to give birth to the disaster is still in power, and implementing policies it was never elected to carry out. The Fianna Fail–Green coalition is immensely unpopular yet, at the start of 2010, it is in power. This is deeply undemocratic. It exposes the current political system as a sham: elections every four or five years of parties backed by the mass media and big money, peddling half–truths and lies. This 'democracy' is the only legitimacy the attacks on working people has, yet this means it has none, for the Fianna Fail-Green coalition was elected to continue the prosperity, not to destroy hope and faith in the future. It has no mandate. To oppose it is therefore to defend democracy.

The government clearly deserves to lose office and every day it stands is an affront to the popular will; for every day that Fianna Fail is in office the programme of austerity is strengthened. This does not mean that there should be illusions in the official opposition; its actions have demonstrated that it is more than happy for Fianna Fail and the Greens to take the unpopular actions that it too would take were it in office. Fine Gael and Labour should replace Fianna Fail as soon as possible only so that they too can be exposed as having the same set of policies. It would be important that both formations be seen to fail within a relatively short period of time so that false alternatives are uncovered quickly. Waiting for the normal course of events to result in a new government has simply been to wait for the new hangman to put on his hood.

General elections would allow the possibility of presenting a socialist alternative and would be justified simply on that basis. An election would allow a debate about how we got where we are and what should be done. But we must be realistic. A socialist majority would not result, and even if it did the economic crisis has revealed that real power belongs to money and those that own and control it. By itself new suits in Leinster House would do nothing to stop the financial meltdown or continuing economic slide. Elections would open up a limited space to advance and organise working people and allow questioning of the system. It is why not only the governing parties but also the opposition have not been clamouring for an election since September 28, 2008, when Brian Lenihan put everything the Irish people own at the disposal of the banks. The opposition parties in the Dail know that they have no fundamental alternative so why come into office and receive the odium that Fianna Fail so richly deserves?

The writer Naomi Klein, in the 'Shock Doctrine', has explained how ruling classes use economic crises to introduce policies that in more settled times could not be justified or imposed. This opening up of possibilities must be seized by those who want to see movement towards a real democratic political and economic system. Working people should recognise the political power that bankers have been able to deploy; able to call immediate meetings of the Government and walk away with promises of over €440 billion, and organise to wield political power that defends their interests. This means striving for real democracy in all areas of economic and political life and creation of a new Republic. It would include, for example, at a very minimum demanding the abolition of all laws that restrict the ability of workers to organise within trade unions, including abolition of the 1990 Industrial Relations Act, plus the undemocratic anti–terrorist and pubic order laws. Democracy at a local level must also have life breathed into it with councils no longer subject to more or less complete domination by central Government or policing and control by city managers. Local councils should immediately be placed in a position to respond to local needs by ending the outsourcing of public services and reverting to local control those already privatised.

Europe and the World

The pursuit of democracy is also required at a European level and the introduction of the Lisbon Treaty is a perfect example of its absence. Rejected by the French and Dutch electorates it was refashioned so that they were unable to vote again and only in the Irish State was a vote possible. When it was also rejected here the vote was taken again. Big business such as Ryanair and US multinationals used money and threats to buy and intimidate a yes vote the second time round. The political establishment united to issue their own threats and promises. Threats that the multinationals would leave if we voted no and jobs would come if we voted yes. After voting yes the multinationals continued to leave and unemployment continued to increase. The Lisbon Treaty will transfer more power to unaccountable institutions which will continue an agenda opposed to the needs of the majority. This has included the judgements of the European Court of Justice, which has undermined hard won rights by allowing companies to exploit lower paid foreign workers in order to undermine local conditions that affect everyone. The Irish people are thus part of a continent wide struggle, which means building links and developing a programme with labour and democratic movements across Europe. The capitalist Governments have come together to push their agenda, it is essential that the working classes of Europe come together in order to counter it.

In the wake of the economic and financial crisis the European Union has been promoted as a means of protecting small nations such as Ireland from the ravages of global capitalism. It has been put forward as an alternative to the 'Anglo–Saxon' model of capitalism existing in the US and Britain, but this is a false distinction – capitalism is a system that encompasses most of the world and Europe is thoroughly integrated within it. Indeed, the EU has been one of the main instruments for promoting the policies of neo-liberalism within its borders and across the world. European financial institutions, and we need only look at Ireland, bear as much responsibility for the current economic crisis as their counterparts in the USA. In fact neoliberalism in many ways is more enshrined in the European Union than elsewhere because the freedom of markets, the liberalisation of capital movement, is enshrined in its very constitution, most markedly through the Maastricht Treaty. During the second referendum on the Lisbon Treaty working people were told that the EU was bailing the country out but this was far from the truth. The function of the EU has been to facilitate Government plans to bail out the banks, not least to protect those German banks to which the Irish owe money.

The real role of the EU towards small nations has been exposed in Greece, which has been the subject of bullying and threats by the biggest European powers demanding yet more attacks on the Greek people's living standards. Far from a mechanism to bail out its weakest members the EU is a mechanism to impose austerity on its poorest, in the case of Greece, in order to protect the rich banks and governments who lent money to the Greek state. The labelling of whole nations as the PIIGS (Portugal, Italy, Ireland, Greece and Spain) is an insult which should be answered by the working people of these nations uniting to defend themselves against the contagion of speculative attacks by the financial markets and austerity from their own governments. The latter have had the full support of the EU, which has threatened to take the lead if national governments are too weak to impose sufficiently deep cuts.

The open threats to governments to maintain fiscal rectitude by unelected bureaucrats in the EU Commission is profoundly undemocratic. Of course these bureaucrats have the support of all the individual governments but there are no democratic mechanisms of any worth in the EU that can be used to check their free–market zeal. An EU governed by a constituent assembly democratically elected by all Europe's citizens with real powers is the only truly democratic proposal within the existing economic framework. A genuine European labour movement is required to unite its members against a common enemy, the more so to combat the narrow nationalism that is used to pit one nationality against another. For example, the often repeated call to every nation to export itself out of the crisis through competitive wage cuts is clearly to the benefit only of the bosses. How on earth could everyone export its way out? Who would do the necessary importing? How could everyone win the race to competitiveness?

The alternative proposed here then is applicable, mutatis mutandis, in every other country, just as the same crisis has affected to varying degrees each and every country. The full realisation of the alternative therefore requires international action by workers just as the existing policies of governments also requires international action by capital and of workers following its instructions. The difference is that in the former the action is to defend jobs, conditions and livelihoods while in the latter the demand is to accept cuts in a race to the bottom which even if it was successful cannot work for the reasons explained – workers of all nations cannot win a rat race for competitiveness.

Financial Crisis

Workers must realise that they bear no responsibility for the banks which are more or less broke; the value of the four biggest fell from €52.8 billion in 2007 to less than €4 billion in 2008. They continue to function only because of the Government's guarantee which really means it is workers' taxes that have propped them up. The guarantee must be repudiated immediately and only the relatively small deposits of the vast majority of citizens protected, just as they were before the guarantee was introduced.

The financial institutions bankrupted themselves through reckless lending which allowed their directors to pay themselves millions in huge salaries and bonuses. During the boom years they were found guilty of tax evasion and overcharging of ordinary customers and now they want the taxes they evaded to bail them out. In 2009, the Irish Times ran a lead story which described Anglo Irish Bank as one that "specialised in large loans to wealthy business figures, including most of the state's larger property developers."[218] There is nothing progressive about its nationalisation and the Government's claims that the bank is of systemic importance reveals their whole bank bailout plan as a cynical lie. The bailout of all the financial institutions has more to do with the cronyism and corruption that would be revealed if any of these institutions were allowed to go under than any concern for the Irish people. Allied Irish Bank and Bank of Ireland are now zombie banks which are of no use to a healthy economy. In fact the banks did little to create the Celtic Tiger boom and much to create the speculative bubble that followed it.

The banks are bust and those who invested in them such as shareholders and bond holders have effectively lost their money. It is not up to working class taxpayers to protect them. They gambled and they have lost. The banks should therefore be expropriated and these investors made to take the loss for their foolish risks. The same applies to those other banks which lent money to these rotten institutions and to the large depositors; both in effect have been investors in banks that took "reckless" risks. Those property

---

218 Government nationalises 'fragile' Anglo Irish Bank, Irish Times, 16/01/09.

developers and speculators who owe the banks money should pay back immediately or have their assets seized. There should be no question of continuing to fund their speculation, as is happening under State supervision, in the remote hope of recovering something far into the future. The Government has allowed many of them to shift the money they had deposited with the banks out of the country while workers are still left with their debts. The Government said, when it announced that Anglo Irish was going to be nationalised, that it would prevent those who owed more than €20 million from taking out the money they had deposited with the bank. It then quickly reneged on this decision.[219] It has continued to bail out the banks by taking workers' taxes to recapitalise them and by buying their bad loans through NAMA. The speculators have taken money from the banks in loans and now want us to pay for them! Seizing their assets will simply allow us to take back what is owed.

The inquiries commissioned by the Government into the crisis do not cover the period of outright state intervention and will not call into question the establishment that presided over the whole economic and political system or the myriad connections between bankers, politicians and developers. Only by opening the banks' books could the truth begin to be exposed. A few workers acting as whistleblowers, a few leaked emails, would do the interests of the citizens of the State a real service by beginning to expose the corruption that workers are being asked to pay for. The working people of Ireland effectively own the banks, and are certainly paying for them, but aren't allowed to know how these institutions created the mess or who is going to benefit from the bail out.

Solution

Capitalist ownership of the banks has failed. Workers must take immediate steps to prevent everyone from being ripped off and to ensure that the money the banks can mobilise is used to develop an economy for the benefit of the majority of the Irish people.

---

219 Irish bank shares plunge, Reuters, 19/01/09.

1. Bank workers must immediately, with the support of their trade unions and the wider union movement, release full details of the bad loans that the Government has demanded we pay for. The PriceWaterhouseCoopers[220] report commissioned by the Government into the banks must be published in full. The exact state of the banks must be revealed to everyone so we know exactly where we stand. These details must not remain the property of the banks or NAMA functionaries. As workers must repeatedly declare – these banks are our property.

2. All workers, in the banks and outside them, must demand that the boards of directors and senior management of all the financial institutions be sacked. Every single one of them is hiding the truth. These boards should be replaced by democratically elected committees composed of bank workers, workers from outside the banks, representatives of the elderly and students, small farmers and small businesses. Local bank branches should have similar committees to guide their work and ensure that they support local economic development. The meetings of the banks should be open to the public so we can all see that they operate to our benefit, so that the criteria for lending is transparent and that they fulfil their promises.

3. The banks must be expropriated and their numbers reduced in the interests of efficiency. Compensation to shareholders should be based on proven need. The loans to the developers and speculators should be reviewed and their assets seized if they are unable or unwilling to pay what they owe. Where these do not cover the loans they owe, both the developers and the banks should be declared bankrupt and new banks established with the assets of the developers, other loans and the existing deposits of workers. State, taxpayers, money should not be wasted in trying to keep the old banks afloat or on NAMA. These will then provide the foundations for the new democratically controlled banks, their infrastructure and funding. The bondholders of the banks' debt, and all the other investors, took a speculative risk, a risk they were warned of, and have lost. They neither deserve nor should receive subsidies by way of compensation. This is what they call capitalism.

---

220 Anglo badly exposed over customer loans, RTE News, 20/01/09.

A similar approach must be taken to NAMA which has become the latest mechanism to transfer wealth from working people to the banks. It should be opposed and an end demanded to a policy of overpaying for rotten loans or other assets. Likewise we should oppose the creation of any additional state debt to pay for the loans, debt that workers will be asked to repay. Workers should let it be known that they will reject all such payment. Since this cannot be achieved directly, not at least until working people have real and direct control over how they are governed, this means opposing and rejecting all the tax increases, wage cuts, welfare cuts, service cuts and service charge increases implemented in order to pay for the debt created. There must be no €5 billion of workers' money given to developers to 'finish' their speculation. If the property speculators cannot pay their debts their assets should be seized in part payment. These assets can assist direct provision of, or funding for, a new development plan. When, after this process, it is clear that NAMA really is a 'bad bank', it should be wound up as bankrupt, with those who invested in it through equity; or through bonds issued by the Government, told that they have also gambled stupidly and they have lost. In effect NAMA, as a bad bank, should be treated just as the other broken banks.

The operation of the agency should immediately be open to public inspection so that we can see by just how much we are being conned into overpaying for the bad loans. This should be the least demanded by the trade union movement and workers should fight for this demand to be taken up. The hundreds of millions of euros saved through ending the lucrative contracts with valuation firms and financial consultancy should be channeled into real economic development. If these experts have anything worthwhile and practical to say on the latter then they might receive some payment, but we suspect it would not earn them as much as their advice on how to waste €54 billion, or however much it turns out to be, on NAMA.

4. The new banks must be placed at the service of the people. A new plan of economic development should be drawn up using the knowledge and creativity of the Irish people plus the energy and imagination of migrant workers. This should be a democratic plan

involving representatives of all working sectors of society including trade unionists, self employed, students and farmers etc.; with advice and assistance from the universities and workers in the economic development agencies of the State. New productive enterprises can be created and funded, providing jobs and wages; owned and controlled by the workers themselves. This will take the place of the funding for property speculation that the capitalist banks were engaged in for over a decade.

A new economy

The Government has trumpeted creation of a new 'knowledge economy' while the State is only ranked 26th out of 28 OECD countries for education spending. [221] It allowed the closure of productive enterprises which embodied real knowledge, such as Waterford Glass and SR Technics. A democratic plan would save these jobs and develop enlarged and new production. The Government and supporters of the private ownership of the means of production argue that only private enterprise can bring back economic growth and prosperity but this has been disproved. Private ownership of the banks did not fund economic development but the building of empty houses where none was needed and half–built offices that will remain unoccupied for years.

The policy of the Government is to push money into the banks in the forlorn hope that the latter will lend, despite evidence from the bankers themselves and the IMF that they would not. Reliance on private capital for economic development is equally unpromising. Multinational investment, even at record levels, was both unable to provide sufficient employment and has always been extremely insecure, demanding a ceiling on wages, prosperity and development before seeking lower cost locations elsewhere. This is not mainly a question of costs or efficiency but of profitability and the locations where most money can be made. Development and security is not to be achieved through competition with lower cost locations in Poland, India or China.

---

221 Education spend lags in OECD report, Irish Times, 10/09/08.

Dell announced the closure of its major operation in Limerick in January 2009 with the loss of 1,900 jobs and will transfer to Poland. But Polish workers are not fools. They know that a company that is shifting production from the coast to inland China to reduce costs will not remain in Poland long.[222] Irish workers hoping for renewed multinational investment should realise that half of the foreign companies which decided to base themselves in the Irish State already regret their decision.[223]

Reliance on the genius of local capital reveals enormous illusions in a sector that has failed despite almost ideal economic and political conditions for success. Irish capital has never favoured productive enterprise when parasitic speculation can offer quicker and easier rewards. The 'success' stories stand out precisely because they are so rare. In 2007, €13.9 billion was invested into European property deals by local capitalists while they couldn't raise €200 million for venture capital projects. No Irish high–tech company has revenue of over $100m and the largest, Iona Technologies, was sold to a US firm.[224]

Even while extolling the advantage of the free market advocates of capitalist economic development reveal their utter dependence on the State. Discussing the possibilities of growth through developing industries based on green energy technologies one author argues that "to get this industry rapidly off the ground will require government involvement with subsidies, pro–green tech policies and a decision to purchase the kinds of fuels and technologies these start–ups will be marketing. This will also greatly assist in getting early–stage venture capitalists interested. The government should consider setting up a green–tech renewable energy research and development organisation and have it take a leadership role in clean energy research, development and deployment, by designing technologies that will allow Ireland to enjoy a growing, prosperous economy while reducing greenhouse gas emissions. The government should also consider instituting loan guarantees to help new green–tech companies get off the ground."[225]

---

222 See Finfacts, November 10 2008.
223 Ibid.
224 Ibid, 24 and 25 June 2008.
225 Celtic Meltdown. Why Ireland is broke and how we can fix it, Cearbhall Ó Dálaigh, The Collins Press, Cork 2009.

The alternative is not to indirectly sponsor individual capitalists or banks which may or may not profitably invest or, in the case of banks, pass on the funding to allow real economic development. The answer is to directly fund economic development that, because it is based on a democratic plan, will involve the maximum number of people and receive the maximum input of ideas and sources of innovation. Democratic accountability can ensure that promises are kept, that lessons are learned from the inevitable mistakes (and successes), that nothing is covered up or well–connected individuals bailed out. Employment and good wages allied with real ownership and control of their place of work are all the incentives that working people require to create and expand productive and socially useful economic development. Availing of the initiative and knowledge of the Irish people can only come about through the cooperation of the whole people, something a system based on exclusive private property in production and competition cannot deliver. Needless to say a corrupt, bureaucratic and incompetent state apparatus cannot do it any more than a crony capitalist class dependent on it.

International

The financial crisis has led to states taking over private sector debt all across the world and replacing it with debt that working class taxpayers are called upon to repay. Financial speculators take bets on how quickly or successfully this price can be imposed, demanding higher interest on loans and bigger bills to be paid if they doubt the ability of governments to impose the necessary cuts. The financial institutions that led the way towards complete collapse of the world–wide financial system therefore hold a gun to the head of those whom they doubt will pay the price. Yet workers everywhere are threatened that on no account should we upset these international financiers without suffering dire consequences such as the inability to borrow to fund state expenditure.

The logic is crazy – we must fund the international finance markets less these markets do not lend to us! But we have seen that even the largest and strongest financial institutions were about to go belly up. That these people are now free to speculate against those whose labour is paying to bail them out illustrates the class nature of the current capitalist system. Working people of every country must refuse to accept the threats of the international financial markets. The crisis has shown that the heads of these institutions were not the 'masters of the universe' that it was claimed they were. They perform functions often with no useful social purpose and often without the slightest idea of what they are doing. In the largest countries of the world the working class could, with relative ease, take over these institutions and allow their operation to fund real economic and social development. Rejecting repayment of loans used to finance pure speculation, which workers had no part in, is a crucial part of an alternative. Low interest rates and speculative lending by European finance created an economic disaster in Ireland. There is no legitimacy to the demand to repay any loans taken out by the Irish State to bail out the speculators who financed the bubble. The cry will go out that the Irish State cannot default on loans taken out and that this will prevent future borrowing if we require it. The answer is that these debts were not taken out by those asked to pay them back, the Irish working class, and that we have no responsibility for them.

The very fact that we do not accept saddling ourselves with billions of euros of debt to shore up zombie banks reduces our need to borrow. The financial markets will not like it but these are the risks they take. The cost of borrowing, should we require it, may go up but it will not be such that it equals the billions being borrowed to fund NAMA. Working people can only take responsibility for the State's debt when they are in a position to determine how much the state borrows, what for and on what terms. It can only accept the bill and how much should be paid if and when it is responsible for the borrowing. Then, workers can and will negotiate with foreign financial markets in their own interests while seeking support and solidarity from the workers' movement in other countries and around the world, pointing them towards taking the same measures as proposed here. The full achievement of a workers' alternative can therefore take place only at an international level when the full power of the financial markets has been broken.

The alternative proposed for Ireland therefore has wider application and the struggle for it is an international one, just as the crisis has been international in scope. While the capitalist solution is competition the alternative is one of solidarity. The idea is well known even if it is seldom fought for at an international level. The alternative put forward is thus dependent not on any technical question of economic functioning – the socialist alternative is perfectly feasible technically, but is dependent on the growth of solidarity across Europe and among workers in the rest of the world. American workers have an interest in Irish workers imposing higher corporate taxation. US workers don't want to see US companies leaving to avail of tax incentives while Irish workers don't want to live in a society incapable of funding decent public services. Of course it will be argued that both cannot gain from the same investment but solidarity can take some measure of control away room the boardrooms whose only interest is profit. It can exercise some control to curb multinationals playing one set of workers off against another. Workers can gain the confidence to realise that they can organise production themselves without waiting for the state to promise subsidies, tax breaks, advance factories, trained workers and guaranteed markets in order to get private capitalists to take other people's money in order to invest.

Ultimately all this can only be successful if workers are able to assert their own ownership over production so that between them they can plan their industry's development to their mutual benefit in all countries. The knowledge to produce resides in workers' heads and the skill to make useful objects exists in their labour. The crisis has shown that the money exists at an international level. The obstacle is private ownership of this money, and of productive assets, and the pursuit of short term gain for a few. The struggle to limit the power of multinationals is a step in the direction of negating capitalist power and asserting the rights of working people. Such solidarity will prevent firms moving to China to undercut wages and conditions while Chinese workers can organise to win higher wages and real public welfare services. That workers across the world have immediate interests in common is clear, what they need are mechanisms to turn these into practical policy. The mechanisms can sometimes start at the national and European levels even while the objective is a world–wide one.

Taxation

The income and wealth of Ireland is notoriously unequally distributed yet even in the midst of a calamitous crisis the State has still protected these inequalities. The bottom half of earners (49 per cent) get just 17 per cent of total income while the top six per cent get 28 per cent. Even after the collapse of share and property values the journalist Vincent Browne has estimated that the top 50 most wealthy are worth €19 billion, or over €380 million each.[226]

Like claims that Ireland has a very generous welfare system, it is claimed that relatively little income tax comes from what is called 'lower and middle income' earners, which is the working class. What this assertion immediately does is ignore the impact of indirect taxation and service charges which are deeply regressive, but in any case Revenue figures purporting to show this are false. So those earning less than €30,000 do not pay only 2.3 per cent of all income tax but 10 per cent, and those earning between €30,000 and €100,000 paid 58.6 per cent of all income tax, not 47.8 per cent. So those earning more than €100,000 do not pay 50 per cent of all tax but 31.4 per cent.[227] That they still pay such a substantial amount is not due mainly to the progressive nature of the tax system but because of huge income inequalities.

That this is so is demonstrated by the enormous wealth these people have been able to accumulate. Even a small tax of 10 per cent on this wealth would raise nearly two billion and a tax of 25 per cent approximately as much as the December 2010 budget. [228] Yet this would affect only 50 people who would still continue to be incredibly wealthy. Instead budgets since the crisis exploded have consisted of much more damaging cuts in the living standards of the vast majority. Yet none of the opposition parties have indicated that they want to do any more than tinker with this approach. Inroads

---

226 Ireland's uniquely steep slump down to us, Irish Times, 29/04/09.

227 Revenue data understate contribution of lower and middle–income earners, Irish Times, 20 March 2009.

228 Ireland's uniquely steep slump down to us, Irish Times, 29/04/09.

into the incomes of the wealthy could go a long way to protecting the majority. Tax relief on private pensions that benefit mostly the top 20 per cent are worth €3.2 billion while other tax reliefs, usually calculated at the higher tax level, include capital allowances, health benefits and the property based incentives which fed the speculative boom.

Figures released by the Revenue Commissioners have shown that several of the highest earners in Ireland paid no tax whatever, while 1,060 with incomes above €100,000 a year paid less than five per cent tax. And these aren't tax exiles – they live in Ireland. It has been estimated that tax not collected on the wealthy could amount to €3 billion a year.[229] The biggest loophole has been the residency rule which stated that someone had to live in the Irish State for more than 183 days a year before becoming liable for Irish taxes on all income. Almost 6,000 people on the Revenue's books declared themselves 'non resident for tax purposes' and 440 'high worth' tax fugitives were estimated to be worth €30 million each.[230] The most blatant tax benefit to the rich of course is the low corporation tax of 12.5 per cent, which means that profits are taxed proportionally far less that wages.

Among the multinationals to benefit most from Ireland's tax regime have been mining and energy companies. While Ireland has valuable mineral and energy resources on land and offshore the Irish people have derived little benefit. The most glaring example of this is the Corrib gas field which has been valued at €9.5 billion, though independent consultants reckon it could be worth up to €21 billion. Despite such wealth within its waters the Irish State will receive very little revenue. Indeed it is actually subsidising foreign energy companies, providing infrastructure and land plus police to act as security and put down protest. Even when the field comes on line the Irish State will have to buy gas at market rates. Up until the mid eighties, when the law was changed, the State got a half stake in oil and gas discoveries. Today the level of tax on the profits of the energy companies in Ireland is only 25 per cent, compared to 78 per cent in Norway and a world average of 50 per cent.[231] Working

---

229 The Tax Dodges of the Rich, SWP, 17/04/09.

230 Budget robs vulnerable to bail out the banks, People Before Profit, 20/04/09.

231 Corrib Gas Go Ahead Granted to Shell – Indymedia Ireland, 27/10/04.

people should demand that the Government immediately renegotiate the Corrib gas field contract, take a controlling stake in the project and increase taxes on profits.

While taxation has a role in paying for the crisis, taxation of the rich is symbolic of a more fundamental change which is required to prevent further crises. The defence of the interests of the majority can only be completed when that majority, primarily workers, gain control over production and the products of their own labour. Ireland's wealth does not derive primarily from what is in the ground or under the sea, or from the profits of capitalists, but from the labour of workers. The fashionable talk of a knowledge economy and of tapping into the initiative of the Irish people is only a distorted reflection of this reality. To really mobilise the initiative, enthusiasm and knowledge of the Irish people requires that it be given, or rather that they take, real ownership of the society it has been called upon to save. Not the fake 'ownership' or 'empowerment' of management theory but real ownership, starting with workers themselves beginning to exercise control over the organisations they work in and over the wealth they create.

Wages and employment

The imposition of wage cuts, put forward by employers and the Government as an essential element of recovery, must be rejected. This is another attempt to pass the costs of the economic crisis onto the working class. It is a myth that wages in Ireland are relatively high, or that high wages are the cause of the economic crisis. The reality is that Irish wages are 25 per cent below the EU average and that wage increases have not been excessive. When the cost of living is taken into account Irish wages have even fallen relative to other European workers.[232]

During the period of the boom the position of the working class in relation to the capitalist class deteriorated. While living standards did increase, the advance of the employer class has been much greater. In this period bosses based in Ireland were making much more in profits than bosses in any other EU economy. For example,

---

232 The Truth About Irish Wages, UNITE, April 2008.

according to the EU's KLEMS database, profits per employee in Ireland stood at an average of €45,800 in 2005, while the average figure for the EU–15 was only €29,500 and €22,500 in the UK. Net profits at enterprise level increased between 2000 and 2005 at more than twice the rate of wages. Net profits per employee increased three times the rate of cost per employee.[233] There has been a huge transfer of wealth from labour to capital. The wage share of national income has gone down from 71.2 to 54 per cent between the periods 1980–1990 and 2001–2007.[234] If anything it is the declining value of wages that has contributed to debt expansion and the financial crisis. Yet the demand from bosses is that wages be depressed even more and that the threat of rapidly rising unemployment be used to enforce this demand.

In order to maintain wage levels and employment it will be necessary first of all to share out the available work without loss of pay. Workers should demand that working hours are reduced with no loss of pay and that the retirement age be reduced to 55, not raised to 68. The minimum wage should be replaced with a 'living wage' – enough to support one adult and one dependent. Deferred wages in the form of pensions must be defended with the creation of a pension guarantee scheme for workers in the private sector. None of these demands that workers must take up can be advanced in the absence of struggle. This is certainly true of the necessity to expropriate companies that cannot guarantee jobs, conditions and wages.

In the December 2010 budget welfare benefits to young people were cut in the hope of forcing them to accept almost any type of job at almost any wage. The mantra of the government, employers and their economic experts is that the level of income received by the unemployed is too high and creates unemployment through pricing workers out of jobs. Campaigns against the level of benefit paid to the unemployed is not confined to Ireland but is seen everywhere. Once again those in work and out of it are compelled to compete with each other. Yet it is no part of workers' demands, or of socialism, that people be paid to do nothing. The very opposite,

---

233 The Truth about Irish Profits, UNITE, June 2008.

234 Ireland government nationalises Anglo Irish Bank while the country faces the second worst recession in the EU, In Defence of Marxism, 28/01/09.

Workers real demand is that they are given work to do and that the State in the first place should have this demand placed upon it. The practice of paying people to do nothing is no part of socialism but entirely rational only for a capitalist society. Only by keeping people unoccupied and on very low income levels is it possible for them to play their allotted role, which is to depress the wage demands of those already in work. That is why there is only one thing worse for the right wing experts than paying unemployed workers reasonable levels of unemployment benefit and that is the state giving them real work at reasonable wages to do worthwhile things. That is why wasting €54 billion in buying toxic loans is considered sensible by economic pundits but spending this amount on an economic development plan is considered outrageous. Yet such a plan would create real wealth, boost economic growth, keep young people from emigrating, significantly lower unemployment and prevent the catastrophic social problems that will result from youth unemployment – demoralisation, delinquency, criminality and drug addiction. If ever a choice was stark this is it, spending money on banks or money on people.

It will be objected that the state is a notoriously inefficient employer, but socialists are not demanding that the sort of bureaucratic system that characterises current state bodies is extended across the whole economy. The rigid, stifling and hierarchical structure of the capitalist state is not a paradise for workers. That many defend employment within it is often because it gives real jobs and provides real services while not being subject to the lash of capitalist competition to the same extent as the private sector. This can indeed reduce efficiency at the level of the individual workplace but the capitalist system has shown that this sort of efficiency is more than offset by economic catastrophe at the level of the economy as a whole. Efficiency at the workplace level can easily be achieved through everyone in it having equal responsibility for effort and performance, with real democratic control and accountability in its management. Regulation can ensure that this is also aligned to the needs of society as a whole. Real democratic planning at the economy level will similarly solve the disasters caused by uncoordinated pursuit of selfish private interest at enterprise and firm level.

What is essential in the current crisis is that workers are active in their own defence and do not accept the bogus arguments about competitiveness and efficiency put up by the Government, bosses and their 'experts.' Competitiveness and efficiency can hardly be advanced by wasting extraordinary sums on banks that are bust, yet that is what these assorted parties claim. What is really involved in this is class rule and class power and it is precisely in crises such as the one now being experienced that this becomes crystal clear. All talk of competitiveness and efficiency only applies to workers not to bankers, not to property developers, and not when it comes to corporate welfare for multinationals.

Housing

The housing policy of the current government has been described as 'social welfare for the rich'. It includes €391m of rent supplement, €169m of tax incentives, €450m of stamp duty loopholes and €400m unspent on local authority accommodation. Housing supply has been determined by a combination of market forces, government tax incentives, and developer led 'planning' rather than any strategic plan based on social need. This policy has resulted in: 56,000 on housing waiting lists, 60,000 depending on rent supplements, 5,000 homeless, 14,000 living in mortgage arrears and also in dispersed, devastated and abandoned communities.[235] What makes this particularly scandalous is that during the period of the construction boom housing supply outpaced need. It has been estimated that between 2006 and 2009 supply outpaced demand by 154 per cent, and that across the country well over 300,000 properties lie vacant. The number of vacant homes greatly exceeds the number of families deemed by the Department of Environment to be in need of local authority housing.[236] An abundance of properties co-existing with rising housing need is a consequence of a system in which houses are assets rather than homes. This is particularly the case in Ireland where property has been the key asset of the credit fuelled boom.

---

235 Tenants First launch an alternative housing programme, SWP, 20/05/09.
236 Failure of government explains social housing need, Politico, 29/01/09.

As it is impossible to separate finance from housing, solutions to the housing problem inevitably follow from the solutions required for the banks. The expropriation of the banks would see new financial institutions take on the ownership of vacant and mortgaged houses. This would include many of the surplus housing units in the country – more that enough to house those currently on housing waiting lists. The vacant houses, if they were suitable, could be transferred to the control of councils as public ownership rental. Overnight the housing waiting lists could be eliminated and families put into decent accommodation. This would save hundreds of millions currently paid in rent allowance to private landlords, which could then be used for other essential public services. Control over financial institutions would make it possible to order a halt to repossessions which are as yet mainly just threatened but which at some point will become a reality for many. Owner–occupiers who are unable to pay mortgages could choose to convert their properties to public rental, or have their homes re–valued and their repayments adjusted to more manageable levels. The revenue accumulated from repayments and rents could be used to fund a programme of council house building, if this is required, or of public infrastructure such as schools, communications technology or proper water and sewerage services. This would allow increased productive employment in the construction sector and provide the opportunity to build and regenerate communities in ways that reflect the needs of the people who live within them.

Health and Education

Despite Government claims that the public sector in Ireland is bloated, the reality is that public spending in Ireland is among the lowest in the developed world and is falling. Public spending as a share of GDP fell from 47.2 per cent in 1988 to 35 per cent in 2008. The Irish State's health spending is way behind that of other European states, accounting for 7.5 per cent of GDP compared to an 8.9 per cent average for the countries of Europe.[237] Much of this is taken up by private medicine and insurance. The State is also spending proportionately less on education than it did 10 years ago. As a proportion of GDP it has fallen from 5.2 per cent in 1995 to 4.6

---

237 Ireland the 'sick man of Europe' for health outlay, Irish Independent, 27/06/08.

per cent in 2005.[238] Many public services are squalid and to bring about improvement will require major investment and restructuring.

The most severe problems are in the health service and are reflected in its entrenched two–tier structure and the distinction between public and private. This is seen most graphically in hospital waiting times as public patients wait years for treatments that private patients receive within weeks in the same public hospital.[239] There are not enough beds available for public patients and, related to this, there is a shortage of medical staff. The ratio of doctors to population is only 22 doctors to 10,000, far below the EU average of 33 to 10,000. Cutbacks in nurse training have also led to shortages. The relatively recent growth in employment in the health service has been biased to the non–medical side, often a reflection of an increasingly bureaucratic system.[240] Another tendency has been the centralisation of management of health services, advanced most in the 2004 Health Act, which abolished regional health boards and created the Health Service Executive (HSE) to control and manage the delivery of all health and personal care services.[241]

The power of private finance has been boosted by successive Governments with medical consultants, for example being gifted public beds in public hospitals for their private practice, many simply ignoring with impunity the official limits on this practice. Taxpayers have been forced to subsidise private medicine, footing over 40 per cent of the cost of for–profit beds. This public–private mix, in which the public is dominated and subordinated to the demands of business, is eating away at the system.[242] Corporate interests, whether as consortiums of consultants, insurance and pharmaceutical companies or private providers of services, have completely penetrated the health service and used it as a mechanism for extracting profit. The number of private nursing homes and private or profit hospitals has increased dramatically, encouraged by the introduction of tax breaks for companies that

238 Amount spent on education falls to third worst in EU, Irish Independent, 10/09/08.

239 Marie O'Connor – Emergency: Irish Hospitals in Chaos, Gill Macmillan, Dublin, 2007, p17.

240 Ibid, p.28.

241 Ibid, p.51.

242 Ibid, p.89.

build or refurbish public or private hospitals and nursing homes. A major push towards privatisation came in July 2005 when the Health Minister announced a new initiative to provide an extra 1,000 acute hospital beds through building private hospitals on public sites, the policy of "co–location". All this means that the service becomes less efficient, less effective and more expensive, which then becomes the excuse for further privatisation and more cuts[243]

There are a number of immediate measures that need to be taken to improve health services. These include: an increase in the number of clinical staff, a major investment in the public health system to clear the problems in A&E; funding of more hospital beds, employment of more specialists to reduce waiting lists; the extension of GP out of hours cover and an end to the outsourcing of hospital catering and cleaning services. To improve accountability all hospitals should be required to publish statistics on medical procedures and their outcomes. All healthcare institutions and personnel should be subject to independent inspection. As a means of tackling staff shortages in hospitals, the gap in medical courses at universities should be lifted, and all medical students obliged to work within the Irish health service for a fixed period upon graduation. A new public only contract for consultants should also be introduced, and enforced, with creation of a common waiting list that would see people treated on the basis of need not income.

A critical condition for even minimal proposals to work is the expulsion of private finance from the health system. If inequalities and distortions are to be removed private health insurers and providers must be abolished. The demand must be for a free, universal, and public health system that covers all required services without charge. Such a system would be funded through a system of national insurance and general taxation. The management structure of the health service must be transformed. The bureaucratic monster that is the HSE must be abolished and the accountability of the health system devolved to the lowest level that is both practical and efficient. Real workers management and control, involving all staff, should be introduced to enforce equality

---

243 Ibid, pp 206 – 10..

of treatment and prevent profiteering while ending the expensive waste embodied in bureaucratic management and the privileged vetoes of top consultants.

Decisions over the delivery of services should be determined by health staff and the communities they serve.

Education

The Irish State comes close to bottom of a recent international league table on education spending, making a mockery of Government claims to want to build a "knowledge economy". According to the OECD's Education at a Glance 2008 report it comes 27th out of 29 countries in the amount of GDP per capita invested in each second–level student. The report also shows that while spending on education increased by more than 80 per cent between 1995 and 2005 GDP more than doubled. During this period, which covered the years of the boom, the proportion of GDP invested in education therefore dropped significantly from 5.2 per cent in 1995 to 4.6 per cent in 2005, while the OECD average stood at 5.8 per cent. Overall, Ireland ranked 30th out of 34 countries in terms of education expenditure as a percentage of GDP. Only six out of 30 OECD countries have a worse pupil–teacher ratio at second level and only two countries, Greece and the Slovak Republic, invest less of their GDP in education. Irish primary schools have 24.5 pupils per class; the second largest of the EU countries surveyed, and on average have four more pupils in classrooms than other EU countries.[244]

The low level of spending is also reflected in the poor physical state of school buildings with many schools having small classrooms, little or no ancillary accommodation, libraries, PE halls or general–purpose rooms. There is inadequate specialist accommodation at post–primary level and many second–level schools, built in the 1970s and 1980s, are of a low cost high maintenance design and are still in use.[245] There are around 40,000 pupils in prefabs and many school buildings are in need of major refurbishment or

---

244 Education spend lags in OECD report, Irish Times, 10/09/08
245 Schools' current facilities in 'poor condition', Irish Independent, 23/06/08.

replacement.[246] These figures attest to the poor state of schools but conditions have deteriorated further through cost cutting budgets. At the end of 2008 it was reported that there had been 32 cuts, 16 of them in the primary sector, which would result in class sizes increasing from 27 to 28.[247] These cuts fall heaviest on pupils from poor and migrant backgrounds. Given such pressures it is no wonder many pupils are being lost to education. Student dropout is currently running at around 20 per cent, which translates into 10,000 students starting second level in any year not completing the Leaving Certificate. The Teachers Union of Ireland has calculated that half of these young people end up on the unemployed register.[248]

The education sector thus urgently needs investment. We need to employ thousands more teaching and support staff in order to bring down the pupil teacher ratio and improve the school experience. Resources should be targeted at pupils who are at most risk of falling out of the system. Every school leaver should be guaranteed a job. A school building programme to improve the physical conditions in which pupils are taught should be rolled out; as well as helping schools this would also serve to boost employment in the construction sector. Schools must be thoroughly integrated into their communities and their management placed in the hands of staff and parents. We need to move away from centralised control of education with its emphasis on arbitrary targets and testing. The current curriculum should be replaced with one whose objective is the realisation of every student's potential. Individual schools should have the freedom to adapt the curriculum and their teaching methods to fit the needs of their pupils. Those that are most successful can provide an example for others to follow. University education should be made available to every student who has the interest and ability to pursue a degree course. There should be no return to student fees. All students who qualify for higher education should receive a living grant. The expertise within universities should be harnessed to the transformation of society, not to partner private pursuit of profit.

---

246 The state of buildings 'must be addressed', Irish Independent, 24/06/08.
247 Groups seek reversal of 'immoral' education cuts, Irish Times, 28/10/08.
248 TUI calculates that student drop-out will cost State billions, TUI, 10/04/09.

Since the inception of the State successive Irish Governments have ceded a large degree of control over health and education services to the churches and religious orders. This has enabled them to solidify their power in society and to use State funded institutions as instruments of religious indoctrination. One of the consequences has been the distortion of practice within health and education: two of the biggest scandals within the Irish health service, the wide use of symphysiotomies in the 1980s and the unnecessary hysterectomies carried out at Our Lady of Lourdes Hospital in Drogheda in the 1980s, were at least partially a consequence of the influence of Catholic doctrine on medical practice.[249] Both practices resulted in the mutilation of hundreds of woman. The Ryan and Murphy reports, as well as the most recent report into the Dublin archdiocese, have provided shocking indictments of the systematic neglect and abuse of children by religious orders and the State. The cosy relationship between State and church has meant that such abuse was covered up for decades. When eventually exposed the State gave immunity to those responsible and protected the religious orders and institutions from claims for financial compensation. The 2002 deal offered by the Government limited religious congregations' contribution to just €127m of an estimated €1.3bn liability with the taxpayer picking up the tab for the rest. [250] Despite their truly shameful record these same institutions remain in charge of children's education.

While compensation for abuse is important, and the compensation deal should be revised and the religious orders made to pay up, it is now most important that the fundamental structure of health and education services is changed. The involvement of churches and religious orders in the delivery of health and education services must end. These services must be completely secular in their structure and scientific in their ethos. The overriding priority of these services must be the physical and psychological well being of the population they serve. In order to achieve this all hospitals and schools must be brought under the democratic control of the workers who staff them and the local communities they serve. Church control is incompatible with democratic control and

---

249 Marie O'Connor – Emergency: Irish Hospitals in Chaos, Gill Macmillan, Dublin, 2007, pp 66 – 68, and p76.
250 Time to separate church and state, SWP, 12/06/09.

transparent accountability. The first step in such a transformation is staff, patients, parents and students rallying to defend their services.

Resistance

Everyone knows that the basic structure of the organised working class, the basic defence mechanism, is the trade union. Yet in recent times, even against the background of stupendous attacks by the State and employers, the trade unions have been in decline and the reasons, as we have shown, are not hard to find. As the attacks have intensified the trade union leaders have adapted. They have adapted with appeals to the policy of social partnership within which they offer collaboration with employers and Government in return for a place inside the tent and an advisory role to the Government. They have claimed that this arrangement is the best that can be got in a bad situation and that, by joining a partnership arrangement, they are best able to protect their members and ameliorate the worst effects of job and wage cuts. The long term result has been a cycle of decay, with relatively fewer and fewer workers signing up to trade unions and the age profile of those active in the unions becoming older and older.[251] In the middle of the crisis the policy of cosy deals with the Government has simply been disastrous, not only for trade union members but for all working people.

So how do workers fight to turn the alternative put forward here into reality? The first thing to say is that there are no blueprints and no methods that guarantee success. There are however certain principles which follow from the alternative policies themselves and that can guide how to think about how to resist. The first is complete independence of working people not only from all the parties committed, in one way or another, to making them pay for the crisis but also independence from the trade union bureaucracy. It has been definitively proved that the bureaucracy stands not with the membership but with the employers and the State.

251 Quarterly National Household Survey, Q2 2007, Union Membership, Central Statistics Office, April 2008.

The first step in dealing with the current trade union officials is to call on them to oppose all talks with the Government aimed at reducing living standards, withdraw from all partnership arrangements and demand recall conferences to adopt a programme of resistance. If and when this fails working people must fight to regain democratic control of their unions by setting up campaigns that seek to impose rank and file control. In doing so workers musts reject the idea that simply replacing old leaders with new ones is sufficient. Democracy has never consisted of simply electing new kings and queens. In taking real control of their unions workers must reject the narrow professional and occupational divisions which trade unions do so much to perpetuate and strengthen. Such divisions have allowed the Government to make some headway in blaming public sector workers for the crisis. Sectional divisions inside the trade union movement should be ignored and a national shop stewards, or rank and file, movement created.

Independence requires working class unity, not just across the various unions but unity with non-unionised workers and with the unemployed, not to mention students, the elderly and those outside the labour force but dependent in one way or another on wages and welfare. It means rejecting divisions based on scapegoating immigrant workers, or the public sector, women or young people. It means opposing nationalist policies which set Irish workers in a race to the bottom against those in other countries through lower corporate taxes (that workers have to make up for) and lower wages. Where there are inequalities in society the working class should fight for these to be reduced, including unequal pay or welfare payments to women or youth. There are no sections of the working class more deserving than any other and unity is only possible on the basis of equality. This means that there are no restrictions to organising solely within the trade union movement because it in no way represents all working people.

Because trade unions are heavily bureaucratised working people have often found it quicker and easier to organise geographically in their communities or around the services they use such as schools or hospitals. The point is that the latter also often lead to divisions, so that health campaigns become simply efforts to save the local hospital, without uniting to save all of them. This localism breeds division which has all too often allowed politicians from the very parties implementing cuts to pose as champions of local services. Across the whole of the country it is easy to see how this is simply a con. Geography becomes yet one more means of dividing working people, division which is the prelude to defeat. Mass campaigns united across the country are thus indispensable in making an alternative a reality. The methods of mass action up to and including a general strike are the only type of weapons that effectively use the power of the majority and threaten the policies and power of the rich and their State.

Unity of those wishing to fight is therefore key, unity inside, across and outside the trade unions. But we must be careful. The call for unity is also often a trap. Too often this call is used by existing union and political leaderships to saddle workers with policies which in no way represent their demands and needs. There is therefore always one question that must be asked when the call for unity is made. Unity for what? Unity under the current leaderships has become a means of stifling and suffocating opposition to the Government. This is because the current leaderships of the trade unions are themselves united, through social partnership, with the Government and bosses. Those that see no problem with uniting with these union leaderships thus find themselves, at one remove, in unity with the very people they believe they are fighting against. The answer to the question – unity for what – must therefore always determine whether unity is necessary and desirable. Breaking with the existing ICTU leaders and of the Dail parties is necessary in order to unite workers around policies that defend their interests.

This short book has set out what these policies look like. The starting point is that workers must resist the attempts to make them pay for the crisis, for the bank bail–out, either through wage cuts or through slashing public services. They should seek to repudiate the debts built up by the bankers and speculators and call for democratic workers control of the elements of the economy that are under threat and are required to maintain jobs and incomes. This alternative then is not one we can call on the Government to implement. It is not one we can rely on opposition parties to adopt and then hope that they will get into office sometime in the future.

It is not one we can leave to union leaders wedded to partnership with those supporting and implementing the cuts. It is therefore one that must created by working people themselves. It is one that goes way beyond simple trade unionism and is political. This socialist alternative requires the support of the majority. No single existing organisation represents this majority and even the largest organisations, the trade unions, are internally divided as we have seen. No amount of democratisation will allow them to unite those outside their ranks, the unemployed, elderly, those in education or otherwise outside the workforce.

The alternative presented here therefore requires a new working class party, one that can provide a vehicle to develop and fight for its application. That can identify and oppose all types of oppression and unite resistance to it. That can develop a political programme that advances the working class to political power, not through election to the current parliamentary system, but through creation of popular and democratic organisations that wield direct economic and political power by working people themselves. One that unites workers irrespective of nationality inside and outside the state; that unites all Irish workers, north and south and which opposes sectarianism, partition and imperialist rule. One that seeks the unity of workers internationally because only on this scale can workers successfully resist, and only on a global scale can socialism be definitively successful. The existence of comparable capitalist institutions such as the G8, G20, EU, IMF, World Bank and World Economic Forums is proof of the international character of economic and political development and of the necessity for international solutions.

The end of the 20th Century was supposed to see the end of socialism. It had become synonymous with bureaucracy and the state, either in Eastern Europe and the Soviet Union or state ownership in the west. More minimally it has been associated with higher taxation and mild redistribution of wealth through increased welfare and progressive taxation. These however have never been the authentic socialist vision and the socialist alternative presented here has not put forward nationalisation as the solution, but workers control and ownership. Nationalisation has been condemned when it amounts to ownership by the capitalist state, which has been altogether reactionary. Demands for nationalisation should only be made to facilitate workers control and ownership and advance their growing direction of economic development. Nationalisation may be demanded in cases of private firms creating redundancies but even here only workers themselves can save their own jobs and develop socially viable and useful activity. Far from relying on the existing state to protect the majority, the crisis has revealed the state as an instrument of the super rich to exploit the working majority. It is not therefore a question of trusting the state if governed by the right party, but opposing it completely and seeking its overthrow and replacement by a real democratic state that embodies the decision making of the majority.

This is the common thread that runs through the socialist alternative, working class control of the banks, health and education services, of firms cutting jobs or conditions, and finally the whole economy. The alternative put forward here therefore presents the original socialist message as one of extreme democracy and working class power. It has presented a revolutionary alternative, one that aims not just at the transformation of society but the transformation of the people who live in it. This is the real purpose of such a socialist programme. It is not to create new institutions, a new economy or even a new state but ultimately to create new people; to make them healthier, more educated, cultured, more secure and happy; to make the needs of people the object of society instead of 'the economy' or 'competitiveness', to which human needs are subordinated. Anger at the gross unfairness and injustice of what is happening today is therefore only a start. It is time to do something about it.

Postscript

"We are not Irish"

This was the slogan shouted by Greek demonstrators on the May Day demonstrations in Athens in 2010. Its meaning was clear. European Union Finance Ministers had decided at the end of 2009 that they wanted "to bounce Greece into Irish–style austerity" and the Greek workers were saying that they would not put up with what the Irish had suffered.[252] Having been the poster boy of the boom the Irish were now being held up as the exemplars of the subsequent age of austerity. But just as the boom was an illusion so the beggar thy neighbour austerity policy made no sense if implemented also in Greece, Portugal, Spain and elsewhere. The crisis in Greece is not only laying bare the crazy logic of aiming to win the race to competitiveness, it is also exposing the role of the EU, which is demanding ever fiercer austerity. Even more fundamentally the crisis has called into question the continued existence of the euro and the European Union itself.

The worldwide financial crisis, driven by the vast expansion of credit and credit products was reflected in Ireland in massive property speculation. In many countries it threatened the collapse of the whole financial system. In order to protect this system the State in many countries substituted itself for the private sector and bailed it out by taking on its debts. The financial collapse, with or without the bailouts, led to a recession that strangled tax receipts in many countries and threatened the solvency of many States. Greece was by

---

252 European Farce descends into Greek tragedy, Wolfgang Münchau, Financial Times 23/12/09.

no means the first to register this fact but, by being the first in the Eurozone to threaten bankruptcy, it also threatened the whole of Europe and, as some financial commentators have worried, the US as well.

The Greek crisis and that of the PIGS (Portugal, Ireland, Greece and Spain) in general has opened up the reality that the EU is not an alternative to the neoliberal model of capitalism but is a leading constituent of it. The EU has acted not to mitigate the crisis but to intensify it, and not because of mistaken policy but because the EU and the euro project have been the prime European neoliberal projects.

Countries like Ireland and Greece have been locked into a common currency with Germany in which adjustments to boost competitiveness have been limited to cutting wages or reducing consumption in general. It is not that Germany is so much more powerful and productive than these countries, although this is true. Rather it is that Greek and Irish workers have not only been subject to pressure on their salaries in the name of competitiveness but so also have Germans themselves. Combined with a high euro exchange rate, workers in the Eurozone have faced the fact that German workers have felt the pressure of low wage labour from Eastern Germany following German unification and the Agenda 2010 labour market reforms. These factors combined have ensured that nominal wages for German workers have hardly risen between 1995 and 2008. Productivity growth of German workers during this period has lagged behind that of Greek and Portuguese workers despite Greek workers being routinely portrayed as lazy spongers. Yet workers in these countries have still failed in the race to competitiveness because German wages have been suppressed. The result for all workers, including the German, who have 'won' this battle for competitiveness, has been a fall in the share of national income going to labour.[253] Even the French reserve currency. This is a second reason to prevent Greek or other defaults as they reduce the real and reputational strength of the euro. This also rules out devaluation of the euro, at least beyond certain limits, and so removes possible routes to

253 Eurozone Crisis: Beggar thyself and thy neighbour, C. Lapavitsas, A. Kaltenbrunner, D. Lindo, J. Michell, J.P. Painceira, E.Pires, J. Powell, A, Stenfors, N, Teles, Research on Money and Finance, March 2010.

restoring competitiveness of countries like Greece. The capitalists of Greece are left with attacking their own workers, but just like their Irish equivalents, they need support to do so and might even hanker after alternative ways to achieve their aims. Hence their support for the EU, which is hailed as their peoples' saviour even while it is the straightjacket that strangles them and limits their options. The latter factor is why the British State has stayed out of the euro.

The Greek crisis has demonstrated that the EU model has failed. The introduction of the euro promised convergence of the disparate economies but this has not happened. The state debt crisis now threatening the cohesion of the EU has raised nationalist fever in which Germans are encouraged to believe that they are bailing out lazy Greeks and Greeks are roused to treat the austerity demanded by the EU as a new Nazi assault. The existing Stability and Growth Pact has failed to protect the euro and those in favour of closer EU cooperation have demanded more stringent mechanisms to ensure compliance. This has included demands to fine errant states or withdraw their voting rights. These undemocratic impulses reveal the rotten core of the EU project.

Solutions

These demands plus the austerity offensive and the €750 billion rescue fund are the immediate solutions of the large business interests and their governments which wish to save the EU project and its ambition to create a great European power. It leaves small states with less and less room for manoeuvre with the Irish State fearful that its low corporation tax is in the frame for harmonisation with taxation in the rest of the EU thereby reducing the advantage of a headline 12.5 per cent rate. That this tax rate is simply the flagship of a policy of attracting mobile international investment that facilitated the crisis is nowhere acknowledged.

The austerity solution however is not an answer even in its own terms. It may or may not be possible to screw down wages in Greece, Ireland and Spain but the imposition of slump economics will not generate a competitive capitalist sector with the technology to compete with Germany or the Netherlands nor lower cost locations in Eastern Europe or Asia. Such a policy promises not a temporary decline in living standards but a necessarily indefinite fall in living standards. It cannot propel the economic growth that alone would drag heavily mortgaged countries out of their debt. In itself such a policy does nothing to prevent financial speculation unleashing another bubble which much weakened states would be unable to repair a second time.

An alternative policy, growing in popularity, recognises all this and calls for poorer countries to do what they have always done and devalue their currency. Devaluation however means leaving the euro, either temporarily or permanently. A temporary withdrawal would be a temporary solution because a once only gain in competitiveness would provide a once only recovery which would dissipate if no more fundamental changes were to take place. Leaving the euro would be a logistical nightmare and would precipitate a flight of capital and leave the newly formed state with large euro denominated debts which it could only default on. Default on debt is therefore an unavoidable corollary of abandoning the euro.

This might seem a progressive course but it is not one that workers should endorse. Its nationalist premise is that the fundamental problem is between nations, between the rich and poor countries of the EU. But as we have seen, German workers have suffered attacks on their wages, on employment and levels of social welfare entitlements in the same battle that now involves Irish and Greek workers. The policy of withdrawal from the euro ignores this and the possibility of a united response by workers all facing the same problem. There is nothing progressive about creation of a new Irish currency. Its value will not be determined within Ireland anyway but by the international financial markets which are at the centre of the problems facing the euro. An Irish currency may have no pretensions to world reserve status but the inevitable devaluation will cut workers living standards just as surely as nominal wage cuts (that is cuts in the money received before taking inflation or the type of currency into account). Such a policy is not an alternative to the austerity demanded by adhering to the euro and the strictures of the EU but is simply another policy option that would involve an equally brutal austerity that would be necessary to defend the value of a new Irish currency.

A third option involves relaxation of the rules governing the euro such as allowing the European Central Bank (ECB) to support States in the same way that it leapt to protect private banks, by allowing it to purchase state debt. This would be supported by a fund which would indicate real solidarity between member states in supporting the financing of each other when the financial markets refuse, or do so only at exorbitant interest rates. A European debt structure could be put in place which raised loans for the EU as a whole and not as exists currently, with debt issued by individual states, so that the creditworthiness of the strong states could be employed for the benefit of the weakest. These mechanisms to consolidate the EU could be expanded by fiscal consolidation; that is expansion of an EU budget that would provide the resources, the tax receipts, to support the most vulnerable countries. The rules of the EU game would change and the strictures of the Growth and Stability Pact would be ditched. In the most progressive model of such a policy new EU wide rules on the minimum wage, unemployment benefits and wage bargaining would be introduced which would stabilise the wage share of the economy.[254]

Some of these steps have been taken, such as the ECB purchasing state debt and the creation of an EU fund to support the credit demands of the most vulnerable countries. Changing the rules of the EU looks less likely, except to tighten them, even if this then exaggerates the most outrageous hypocrisy. So the German State wants extra safeguards to prevent poorer countries getting deeper into debt, thus endangering the value of the euro, while German banks simultaneously lend money to these vulnerable states. The circle is completed when the German State bails out the German banks and blames Greek workers for paying themselves too much while it simultaneously bears down on German wages. German banks are thereby encouraged to make risky loans while poor debtors are screwed.

At the end of the day the creation of the EU and the policy of a strong euro are part of a global competition with the US and emerging world powers such as China. It would be impossible to weaken the forces compelling ruthless competition within the EU, say between German

---

254 Eurozone Crisis: Beggar thyself and thy neighbour, op cit.

and Greek or Irish capital, while pursuing this competition on the world stage. It would equally be impossible to seriously limit the freedom of financial markets within Europe if a strategic objective is the projection of the euro as a world reserve currency with more or less complete freedom for it to move or for financiers to buy and sell euro assets.

Thus the barrier to the idea of changing EU rules to ones that guarantee labour rights, or living standards, or a wage share of the economy, is not the existing rules but the rules of capitalism itself. These demand as a matter of economic necessity, not EU law, that capitals compete as hard as they can and that the weakest go to the wall so that the strongest can aggressively accumulate yet more capital. In this process money for investment by the financial markets must be free to make more money either by investing in the prospective winners of this competition or betting on what the consequences for securities, currencies and sovereign debt will be from success or failure. That this translates into whole countries facing bankruptcy is almost as inevitable as individual companies losing out and becoming bankrupt.

Under the existing framework however whole countries going to the wall can only become analogous to individual firms going bust if the EU becomes more than a collection of states and becomes one super-state, within which purely regional parts may suffer regression and failure but no threat to the integrity of the state as a whole is possible and no destruction of the legitimacy of the form of political rule is entailed. In a capitalist system that guarantees unequal development resulting from unplanned and chaotic competition no voluntary unity of states is possible under any conceivable set of rules that would guarantee equality and freedom of its component parts. It must be remembered that the EU was originally a common market; that is an area in which the barriers to trade and the free market were steadily to be removed. The credit crunch and resulting recession have shown at a global level that the free market is unstable and prone to crisis. Thus the undoubted need for international cooperation at the European level has driven forward the geographical extension and deepening of the EU but cannot overcome the contradiction between the emergence of an international economy of multinational manufacturing and cross border finance institutions and the nationally limited states that regulate, protect and legitimise the system.

Forward?

This analysis has two implications for working people seeking an alternative. First, that the forces of economic chaos that caused the recession are not primarily national even if national factors determined the specific characteristics of the recession: a property bubble in Ireland and Spain and a fiscal crisis of the state in Greece. It was German, British and French money that fuelled the credit boom in Ireland and it is EU rules that prevent controls on such money. It was not the Irish economy as such that led Pfizer to sack hundreds of workers in Ireland at the end of May 2010, as Government ministers were so keen to explain, it was the forces of international capital. No purely national solution is therefore possible.

The second is that the rules of the EU can only be changed if European unity has a completely different purpose other than creation of a free market for capital, for money, for speculation and for exploitation. An alternative European unity that sought not to facilitate competition between German production and Irish or Greek industry, but sought their complementary development in a society of around 500 million people would create a powerful force for good[255] Instead of creation of unsustainable debt among the poorest states the money that exists could finance development of an economy that met the needs of its citizens. It is now abundantly clear that the barrier to creation of a cooperative economy is not shortage of money. If it is not obviously one of a shortage of resources either, it is clearly the way these are combined and organised in a capitalist economy that is the problem. The creation of a cooperative Europe, one of solidarity between its citizens, is only possible in a society built out of equality and freedom, a united socialist states of Europe in which the workers of the continent work together to ensure, for example, that if German workers can efficiently produce cars then Greek or Irish workers can produce other goods and exchange their production in conditions of equality.

---

255 Eurostat, Data in focus 31/2009.

These principles of solidarity and equality are inimical to free market capitalism which is the purpose of the EU. The EU is not therefore the solution but one important element of the problem. The demands raised to deal with the economic crisis in Ireland set out in this book are applicable across Europe. Workers ownership and control of the banks and finance system plus planning of the economy apply with even greater force in a Europe of 500 million which already has the resources to dramatically improve the livelihoods of its people. Just as in Ireland it will take the creation of a new workers' movement, conscious of the international nature of its politics and opposed to all manifestations of narrow nationalism, to make this a reality. It will take a conscious effort to create such a movement, which can start by organising international action against the common attacks perpetrated by the EU across Europe. A common international enemy makes it obvious that a common international response is required.

For Irish workers the crisis of the last few years will provide lessons that there is something radically wrong with the existing economic and political system. For the many who fail to draw the necessary conclusions the efforts of the same system to fix its problems will provide further opportunities to learn. The crisis ridden character of capitalism will continue to provide them with new lessons. The crisis in Greece and its extension to other countries will also demonstrate that this really is an international problem requiring international solutions. Even the most minimal resistance comes up against the charge that we cannot buck the financial markets, the same ones we are saving!

We therefore end where we started. Events will confirm the socialist analysis of the system we live under. It will be those who claim capitalist policy is irresistible who will be less and less in tune with reality. Workers can rally to the socialist cause with the knowledge that it is powerful because it is true.

www.ingramcontent.com/pod-product-compliance
Lightning Source LLC
Chambersburg PA
CBHW021832020426
42334CB00014B/596